Another school is possible

TERRY WRIGLEY

Bookmarks Publications & Trentham Books

Terry Wrigley is a senior lecturer in education at Edinburgh University. He is editor of the journal *Improving Schools* and has previously published two books, *The Power to Learn* (Trentham, 2000) and *Schools of Hope* (Trentham, 2003). He is a member of the Scottish Socialist Party and active in Stop the War. He is also a founding member of the Rethinking Education network.

Another school is possible
© Terry Wrigley
Published July 2006
Bookmarks Publications, c/o 1 Bloomsbury
Street, London WC1B 3QE
Trentham Books, Westview House, 734
London Road, Stoke on Trent ST4 5NP
ISBN: 1905192134

Printed by Cambridge Printing
Illustrations by Tim (www.timonline.info)
Cover photos: Jess Hurd/reportdigital.co.uk
Cover design: rpmdesign
Layout design: mindfield-design.org.uk

Contents

Introduction

Our world is in poor shape. The icecaps are melting, the waters rising and poisons are spread across the earth. A holocaust of poverty, hunger and preventable disease kills 30,000 children each day. The war for oil is turning Iraq into a living hell and the warmongers have further conquests in their sights. The scale of poverty and injustice is monstrous – globally and here at home.

It is increasingly clear that these issues are connected. Ecological disaster, poverty and war are actively produced by the forces of capitalism. The world's owners, relentlessly chasing profits, are acting as if there is no tomorrow:

> Its owners treat the planet as if it could be discarded, a commodity to be used up... But what other world are we going to move to? Are we all obliged to swallow the line that god sold the planet to a few companies because in a foul mood he decided to privatise the universe? *Eduardo Galeano*[1]

This is the context in which we can begin to understand the crisis facing our schools. The World Bank sees education as a means of producing "human capital". We see education as an opportunity to make sense of the world. Our global masters don't want that – it would be far too revealing.

Capitalism has always had a problem with education. Since the Industrial Revolution and the early days of mass schooling for working class children, the ruling class needed to increase the skills of future workers but was terrified that they might become articulate, knowledgeable and independent-minded.

Early in the 19th century the religious philanthropist Hannah Moore justified the founding of Sunday Schools:

> They learn, on weekdays, such coarse works as may fit them for servants. I allow of no writing for the poor. My object is...to train up the lower classes in habits of industry and piety... Beautiful is the order of society when each, according to his place, pays willing honour to his superiors.[2]

Throughout the Victorian period, policy documents said bluntly that you mustn't educate working class children beyond their station in life. The elementary schools were set up to teach basic literacy and numeracy, to discipline children into the rhythms of factory life, and to instil pride in the British Empire – though some teachers always struggled to overcome these constraints.

Times have changed, but the basic principle remains: capitalism needs workers who are *clever enough to be profitable*, but *not wise enough to know what's really going on*. In effect, two factors complicate this. First, employers have different views of what they need: some insist on "back to basics" – more spelling practice and multiplication tables – while others, more forward looking, would like communication skills and initiative, but not too much of it. Second, there is a belief among teachers that schools should do more than prepare young people for work – a more democratic and responsible vision.

The period from the 1960s to the 1980s saw many attempts to develop a more meaningful curriculum – one that could give all young people access to learning and help them achieve a critical understanding of the world. In 1988 Margaret Thatcher's Conservative government imposed a National Curriculum to block all that. The National Curriculum seemed a perfect solution for capitalism – technologically advanced but socially reactionary. On the one hand, it enhanced maths and science, and introduced design and technology, and IT – though it carefully avoided critical thinking about the social impact of science and technology. On the other hand, it provided no opportunity to study modern society and politics, while in English and history it placed more emphasis on national traditions than on multicultural perspectives. It was, however, based on the principle of a broad entitlement for every pupil, and opportunities remained for socially committed teachers to include critical thinking on issues such as environmental concerns in science and geography, or the mass media in English lessons.

What Labour's Tony Blair has done since is far worse. The principle of a "broad and balanced" curriculum in secondary schools has disappeared. His 2006 Education and Inspections Bill makes it clear that only a minority of young people will follow a broad range of subjects. From age 14 or even earlier, most will have a staple diet of job training plus "functional" literacy and computer skills. These pupils, destined for basic manual and service sector jobs, will no longer be entitled to study subjects such as history, geography, design and technology, another language, drama, art, media or music. In effect, Blair's government is creating an upper and a lower division of secondary education.

In England and the US, the heartlands of neo-liberal reaction, childhood itself is being consumed. Children are tested to destruction, and learners stuffed with fragments of dead knowledge like turkeys for Christmas. Despite the government's rhetoric of "raising standards", learning is being trivialised.

Literacy is treated as a mere exercise, disconnected from pleasure and purpose, and knowledge is "delivered" in the straitjacket of governm ʳ-approved lesson plans.

In the 20 years before the 1988 Education Reform Act, teachers introduced important changes in many schools – learning through play and creative activities for younger children, topics for investigation, working in groups, encouraging learners to express their ideas and feelings. These progressive reforms have largely been rolled back under sustained government pressure. Children have been reduced again to passive listening or giving short answers to teachers' questions.[3] Even when government advice seems to encourage interaction and cooperative group work, this is undermined by the constant pressure to increase pace and test results. The result is an assembly-line style parody of interactive learning – cooperative discussion disciplined by a stopwatch.[4]

The two decades before 1988 also saw the widespread introduction of comprehensive schools and the struggle to establish a multicultural and nti-racist curriculum. Since then we have seen the erosion of the comprehen 've principle through market competition and covert forms of selection, aɪ a standardised curriculum that has marginalised minority cultures.

It doesn't have to be like this. Teachers, students and parents can fight back. Indeed, many teachers persist with more enlightened methods, despite the bureaucratic overload or the nagging worry that inspectors from the Ofsted education watchdog might catch them out. Collectively, through trade unions and curriculum or primary associations, teachers have made a united voice heard and confidence for action has grown.

It is helpful to look at schools across the world that have managed to provide more meaningful learning. A shining example is the US teachers' network Rethinking Schools,[5] which inspired a group of teachers to set up Rethinking Education here.

Rethinking Schools combines two roles: it campaigns against reactionary government policies and it publishes radical but very practical ideas for the classroom. In Britain, Rethinking Education was launched in March 2005, with more than 230 teachers, parents, students and school governors attending its inaugural conference. Building on the strength of the NUT (teachers' union) and UCU (lecturers' union) branches and the Anti-SATS Alliance campaign against testing, it will help to develop creativity and courage through working together.

In particular, it can provide an alternative vision for the generation of new teachers who have been trained to think that government strategies and lesson plans from the Department for Education and Skills are all there is. A crucial task will be to bring together curriculum associations, union activists and schools that have dared to swim against the tide to develop a more powerful voice and intervention. This book, like the Rethinking Education website www.rethinkinged.org.uk, aims to encourage more exciting and engaged teaching by sharing good ideas.

It will also help spread news about innovative schools in other parts of the world. Given the strength of the government's stranglehold, we can learn from countries with more democratic educational traditions, such as in Scandinavia where the neo-liberal reform of education has less of a grip.

Resistance is growing. The Norwegian pupils' union saw the introduction of tests as a way of setting up league tables, unfair competition between schools and privatisation. When the union organised a boycott of national tests, a quarter of 15 year olds handed in blank sheets of paper, forcing the Norwegian government to abandon this kind of testing. An alliance of parents, teachers and students has organised massive protests in Italy, while the struggle against city academies and the proposed trust schools has taken off in England.

Policy makers in England are increasingly isolated from other parts of Britain. The Welsh Assembly is reducing the burden of testing and there are widespread demands to open comprehensive schools in Northern Ireland. Education in Scotland is pulled both ways, between imitating Westminster's New Labour policies and a more democratic and independent impulse. Scotland's new curriculum reform plan, A Curriculum for Excellence, cuts back the required content to allow scope for creative activities and in-depth learning.[6] The success of this project will help to undermine the fortress of the English school system. It is not possible in a short book to reflect these different situations adequately, but readers outside England will hopefully find the book a help in developing a more specific analysis and course of action.

Finding a space for real learning is a challenge, but one that we cannot shirk. Critical and more engaged thinking about science and history, media and the environment must be at the heart of curriculum change. Critical literacy, including media education, should count among the new basics of education for a 21st century democracy. Another world is possible. Because of that, another school is possible – and very necessary.

The book has two main sections. The first shows the consequences of government policies. Chapter 1 is about testing, the engine used to drive the whole machine. Chapter 2 looks at the other ways in which schooling is controlled by the government. Chapter 3 questions the dominant models of educational change, known as School Effectiveness and School Improvement. Chapter 4 is about the defence of comprehensive schools and opposition to privatisation, including city academies and the proposed trust schools. Chapter 5 focuses on some of the most vulnerable young people in this education system, including school exclusions and the epidemic diagnosis of "attention deficit hyperactivity disorder" or "ADHD".

The second part, with the appendix, has a more positive slant. It describes many inspiring examples of caring schools and interesting learning. Chapter 6 asks how schools can become more enjoyable and more democratic. Chapter 7 explores more exciting and critical versions of literacy outside the approved model. Chapters 8 and 9 present a rich set of ideas on teaching and learning, and particularly their contribution to citizenship. The conclusion provides a short history of the recent struggle for education and some suggestions on what lies ahead. The appendix describes two highly innovative schools, in Germany and Spain – not as blueprints, since every situation is different, but as an inspiration to show what can be achieved.

Throughout the book there is a deep concern with young people who are growing up in poverty or encountering racism. But this book goes much wider: the global concentration of wealth and power affects us all and raises major challenges for schools, the curriculum and teaching.

Despite appearances, books are never just written by individuals, and many people have contributed knowingly or unwittingly to this volume. I wish to thank in particular Pete Cannell, Jane Bassett, Alasdair Smith, Jim Aitken, Nick Grant and Moira Nolan, who read various drafts and who made many helpful comments, along with Jon Berry who provided most of the material for the Conclusion.[7]

The book's first source is the day to day work of countless teachers who have dared to take risks. It stems from their stubborn refusal to see teaching as a slavish or enslaving activity. By working together in schools and through curriculum organisations, conferences and publications, they have kept real education alive.

Its second source is the struggle of union members against reactionary government policies such as league tables, selection and performance related pay, often joined by parents and the wider community. Needless to say, many active members of the NUT, UCU and other unions combine a vigorous public defence of education with creativity in the classroom.

This book owes a considerable debt to engaged university teachers and researchers for their integrity and persistence. The major sources are acknowledged at the end of the book, along with suggestions for further reading.

Finally, the struggle for education is not separate from a wider cultural and political struggle. It goes on in parallel with campaigns to defend other public services such as the NHS, pensions and council housing. Trade unions in many industries are finding a new spirit of resistance. The anti-war movement, environment and global justice campaigns and the anti-capitalist movement across the world are stimulating teachers and young people to make better sense of the world and to take responsibility for changing it. We are at a critical but hopeful point in history.

Together, our voices will be stronger and our efforts will bear fruit. We can overcome the limitations of today's schools. Through collective struggle we can fulfil our dreams of a better education and a better world.

Part one:

What is happening to schools?

CHAPTER 1

Tested to destruction

Poor assessment undermines good teaching and learning, and distorts the curriculum. There is a growing consensus about the harmful effects of testing in England and the machinery of surveillance that has been built on it. Once more, Tony Blair and his ministers are the last to understand this.

The English education system is obsessive about testing. It could win an Olympic gold medal. The problem is not only the expense and the number of tests pupils sit, but the insidious ways that test preparation and a testing mindset have come to dominate teaching and learning. It pervades the entire life of schools and is deeply corrosive of real learning.

The government argues that, without the tests, the most deprived children would fall behind. The opposite is nearer the truth. Former Ofsted director of inspection David Taylor told the House of Commons Education and Skills Select Committee that tests were creating a new 11-plus effect by making pupils who did not get the grades believe they were failures.[1] Working class boys in particular had become the "unwitting casualties" of the testing regime, which put them at risk of becoming disaffected and disruptive at secondary school.

Children's lives at primary school are dominated by the school's need to get high scores. This particularly affects schools in poorer neighbourhoods, which are under greater pressure to hit targets, while schools in better off areas can afford to be more daring and original and provide a richer education. In 2003 more than 80 children's authors and illustrators joined a campaign calling for an end to national tests. Teacher and author Alan Gibbons said:

> Parents buy revision packs rather than books... National tests have squeezed storytelling in schools. Many junior schools have stopped having story time at the end of the day.

The literacy hour, introduced in 1998, gave little priority to reading for pleasure or for real purposes. A survey by the National Foundation for Educational Research found that children now enjoyed reading less.[2] The Schools Health Education Unit, an independent research organisation, reviewed children's lifestyles, leisure and wellbeing, and discovered that the proportion of ten year old boys who read books at home nearly halved during the first five years of the national literacy strategy. This shows a tragic short-sightedness by narrow minded policy makers. As international data has shown, levels of achievement at age 15 depend largely on whether or not young people have come to enjoy reading.[3] The studies concluded that enjoying reading in your spare time is an even more significant factor than socio-economic background. The research also shows that reading newspapers, magazines and comics can be as effective as reading books, and that parents can help boost literacy skills by discussing books, articles, politics and current affairs.

Even the official evaluations of the literacy hour in England, by school inspectors and a specially appointed research team from Canada, show how testing is damaging the rest of the curriculum, with teachers spending more and more time on subjects that are tested.[4] They also argue that the high-stress accountability regime is causing overload and driving teachers out of the profession.

One of the corrosive effects of testing is that it turns learning into an exercise – mere practice for the test. Children are constantly being told to learn something because they will need it in the test. This results in a very different attitude to learning than when we find out about something because it is interesting. It is not a sustainable way to "raise standards", quickly leading to boredom and to pupils doing just enough to get over the next hurdle.

Do SATs tell the truth about achievement?

The government constantly uses rising test scores as evidence that its policies are working, but recent research casts doubts on these claims. Some damning reports in the *British Educational Research Journal* suggest that SATs cannot be trusted.[5]

The national numeracy strategy imposed particular ways of teaching maths, emphasising whole-class practice of mental arithmetic. The strategy cost £400 million, but researchers say it has led to pupils gaining numeracy skills only two months faster than before – and perhaps led to a deterioration in mathematical skills other than calculation. Professor Margaret Brown and her colleagues at King's College London point out:

- Two thirds of schools showed progress, but results went down in the rest.
- Results got worse for low-attaining pupils, probably because teachers were now focusing on the children in the class with average levels of attainment and no longer paid attention to the needs of those who were struggling most.
- The gap increased between the lowest attaining pupils and the rest.
- There was little improvement for the most advanced pupils.[6]

Some high attainers…expressed to us their frustration at their progress being held back by the whole class teaching emphasis, which tends to be pitched at the needs of the middle of the group.

The government claimed that the number of 11 year olds reaching the target level 4 in maths had risen by 14 percent between 1998 and 2002. The researchers queried the spin doctors' choice of 1998 (an unusually poor year) as a baseline. The more appropriate start date of 1999 (the year immediately before the numeracy strategy was introduced) would have shown only a 4 percent improvement. The researchers also argued that improved SATs scores were partly the result of careful coaching for the test.

Durham University's curriculum, evaluation and management centre is highly rated for its expertise on assessment. In its August 2004 report, Professor Peter Tymms questions how much reading standards are actually rising.[7] He compares SATs results with data from 11 other sources, including government departments and universities. This data includes some very stable tests – as opposed to SATs, which keep changing – and a very large sample of nearly half a million pupils.

Tymms concludes that the SATs have been simplified. He suggests, as a fairer estimate, that the proportion of pupils genuinely reaching level 4 rose from 48 percent in 1995 to about 58 percent in 2000, rather than the 75 percent shown by the SATs.

After 2000 little change occurred in the results. In fact, the biggest change in scores occurred before the literacy hour was even introduced. It seemed to make no difference whether pupils had followed the literacy hour for one year or many – after rising suddenly in 1999 and 2000, the percentage reaching level 4 stayed at 75 percent in 2001, 2002 and 2003. Pupils sitting the tests in 1999 only had the literacy hour in their final year at primary school and those who did the tests in 2000 had literacy hours only in the last two years, but these pupils did as well as those in 2001 to 2003 who had been given literacy hours for longer. Where is the advantage of subjecting children to the literacy hour throughout primary school?

When the SATs were tried out on pupils in Northern Ireland, who have a different system of education and had not been coached for the SATs, the pupils immediately spotted that they were getting easier.

Cambridge University lecturer Mary Hilton has shown exactly how the tests were made easier.[8] She discovered that the government's official qualifications body, the Qualifications and Curriculum Authority, had changed the criteria. There were more straightforward factual questions and fewer that required interpretation and reading between the lines. There was a switch from more subtle questions involving inference or deduction – understanding something that the writer has hinted at rather than directly stated – making it easier to classify readers who were still struggling as having reached level 4. The most dramatic year on year improvement in SATs scores coincided with a shift in the text used in the test from an author's thoughtful personal account of her childhood (1998) to much simpler passages about spiders (1999).

Simplifying the tests in this way allows the government to claim that its policies are working. At the same time, teachers are getting better at judging exactly what they need to teach to get children through the tests. The QCA admits this. Its own research reveals that many children are spending two hours a week doing practice tests.

An official evaluation carried out by Ofsted pointed to an increase in basic exercises rather than meaningful reading.[9] It called them "holding activities [which] occupied pupils but did not develop or consolidate their literacy skills" and resulted in reduced interest and motivation. Ofsted found:

- Some schools had abandoned independent reading, which didn't fit into the official pattern of the literacy hour.
- Boys were responding badly to one lesson in eight (even under the inspectors' gaze) and the gap between boys and girls was not closing.
- The curriculum was narrowing, as teachers focused more and more on the tests.
- The development of enquiry skills in history and geography and the refinement of technical skills in practical subjects were "being neglected".

Ofsted suggested that teachers should connect reading with real knowledge in subjects such as history and science – just as many primary teachers used to do before the testing regime.

Now two of England's greatest experts in science teaching and assessment, Michael Shayer and Paul Black, have discovered that 11 to 12 year olds are "now on average between two and three years behind where they were 15 years ago" in terms of cognitive and conceptual development. Teaching to the test is leading to superficial learning, without any real understanding of the underlying concepts.[10]

A different spin on the results?

The problem doesn't stop at age 11. According to the OECD's PISA international tests in language, maths and science for 15 year olds, British schools are doing well overall, but with a large attainment gap between high and low achievers.[11] The connection between low achievement and poverty is greater than in most other countries. This is a serious issue: when you are looking for a job or a university place, your achievement relative to others in your own country matters more than any international comparisons.

This gap showed up very clearly in GCSE results – until two years ago. It appears to be closing lately, but a closer look reveals a flaw in the statistics. A GNVQ (intermediate level) qualification is now counted as "equivalent" to four higher grade GCSEs. Many schools serving poorer neighbourhoods, after being threatened with closure if they didn't raise their game, switched large numbers of pupils to GNVQs in computing. They were able to buy internet-based tuition and enter pupils for online assessments, which could be repeated until they passed.

Nearly half the pupils in the government's list of "100 most improved schools" follow this GNVQ course, compared with a national figure of one in ten pupils. There are undoubtedly schools on the list that have achieved a dramatic improvement, but in many, actual GCSE results have hardly changed at all. This is not to blame the schools – they made a tactical decision under extreme pressure. Schools have been forced to find ways round the system rather than putting young people's needs first. As more and more schools adopt this strategy, however, it has a general effect of narrowing the school curriculum.

This pressure to get exam results up, by any means, is one of the reasons behind reduced numbers of pupils studying A levels in maths and the sciences. Schools and colleges often deter potential students in case they get lower grades, which would bring down the institution's average.

Amazingly, the equivalence between an intermediate GNVQ and four GCSEs at grade C or above has never been checked by either the QCA or Ofsted. My own scrutiny of results suggests that it is far easier to get a GNVQ intermediate qualification than an A* to C grade in GCSE English or maths. In schools where many students take GNVQ, only half of those who pass it gain a GCSE grade C or above in English, with similar results in maths. In some schools, every student with a GCSE grade E in English or maths managed to pass at GNVQ intermediate level. [12]

There was uproar after the 2004 exam results when newspapers discovered that a distinction in a vocational cake decorating course would count for more than an A grade in GCSE physics. Protests forced the government to introduce a new measure of schools' achievements. This counted the number of pupils gaining five or more good GCSEs "or equivalents" only if GCSEs in both English and maths were included.

The government has dismissed critics of the vocational courses as "old-fashioned elitists". But this is New Labour spin. Work-related courses are valuable as part of a broad and balanced curriculum for all young people, but not when a vocational course simply replaces other important learning. We also have to ask about the "exchange rate" of this new currency in the real world. How will employers and colleges judge people with these qualifications? Can Ahmed, with his GNVQ computing certificate and one GCSE, compete with Robin who has five good GCSEs and computer skills as well?

NATIONAL TARGET

Let us imagine what happens to Jasmine, with a cake decorating qualification and a computing certificate officially worth four GCSEs. With her delicacy of hand and newly won self-esteem, she decides to become a brain surgeon – but which university will take her on? Students like this are being cheated by the government's spin – phoney egalitarianism at the expense of the most disadvantaged young people.

We have to be wary of the elitist right wing chorus that "more students gaining qualifications means standards have fallen". That is not what is being argued here. In fact educational standards may be rising, although less than the government claims. The issue here is the government's misuse of test and exam statistics to claim that its policies are working – spin rather than genuine improvement.

Meanwhile other kinds of educational achievement are neglected. A recent survey of 26 European countries showed that British pupils were the second poorest at speaking a second language. Scandalously, those young people who speak languages such as Bengali and Arabic at home receive very little support in developing their skills.

The impact on working class and ethnic minority learners

The constant push to raise exam results at age 16 has hidden a very important fact: the scandalous neglect of large numbers of 16 to 19 year olds. A quarter of 17 year olds receive no full or part-time education or training. According to the OECD, this puts Britain 25th out of 29 industrialised countries.[13] In eight European countries more than 90 percent of 17 year olds are continuing their education, while in Finland, Norway and Sweden 90 percent are still in education at age 18, mainly full time. Britain's poor record is likely to be due to a combination of factors: employers' neglect of young workers, a sharply divided society with high levels of poverty and an education that many pupils simply find boring.

Britain, alongside the US, has one of the widest social divisions in educational attainment. This is because the gap between rich and poor in society at large is greater than in most developed countries, and because the link between school achievement and family background is stronger than elsewhere.

Our schools also divide pupils into different "ability groups", sometimes from the age of five. Pupils growing up in poverty, whose parents are less well educated, or who speak little English at home, tend to be placed in "low ability" groups. These groups are likely to have a less interesting curriculum, based heavily on dull and repetitive exercises without any meaningful context or purpose.

Neo-liberalism and testing

According to neo-liberal economics, there is nothing that a national government can or should do directly to interfere with the economy. Supposedly, everything is down to market forces. We can understand the obsession with testing in part by attempting to relate it to neo-liberalism in theory and practice.

1) Neo-liberal politicians such as Blair use inflated test scores to demonstrate their country's suitability for investment. They claim that employers will gravitate towards a well qualified workforce to boost their profits. There are a number of a problems with this claim, however. First, there is no evidence to show that things really work this way. Second, there are other reasons why investors might be attracted to Britain, such as its low wages and limited workers' rights – until the employers find even lower paid workers to exploit in India and China.

Thirdly, even in advanced "knowledge economies", capitalism seems to require large numbers of low-paid, low-skilled workers as well, filling jobs in a service sector that under-uses the average school leaver's skills and knowledge. (This might be one of the reasons for a sharp change in the direction of government policy, towards a clear division of learning into academic and vocational tracks – see Chapter 4.)[14]

2) "League tables" of school test results accelerate the market competition between schools. In the 1980s Tory prime minister Margaret Thatcher claimed that competition would wipe out less effective schools and raise standards – the survival of the fittest. The truth is that the increasing divisions between schools serving different areas match the increasing social divide in a neo-liberal economy.

3) The neo-liberals' adherence to the free market is to some extent a flag of convenience. They are perfectly ready to use military force to seize a country's oil and mineral wealth or to use the police to break strikes. Similarly, the government is good at manipulating evidence as a pretext for closing schools in order to reopen them as privatised academies.

4) Just as neo-liberal ideology, with its accountancy mindset, emphasises economics at the expense of politics, a test-based education system reduces everything to numbers. The "use value" of learning, including the learner's satisfaction at developing new skills and understanding, means less and less; and the exchange-value (test scores as a kind of monetary reward) dominates their conciousness. In a consumerist society, we come to see the price of everthing and the value of nothing. The only real thing that matters is literally what you can count.

5) Testing takes attention away from other aspects of the curriculum, including arts and humanities, and political concerns such as the environment, world poverty or equality. Such matters are considered an obstacle to single-minded profit making – and are surplus to requirements in a lean utilitarian vision of education.

There is another way

Assessment is not in itself an evil. Some forms of assessment give valuable feedback on learning. Evidence from assessment – not necessarily test scores – can be used to identify and deal with underachievement, for example among African-Caribbean or white working class students. Some assessment is necessary to demonstrate that specific knowledge and skills have been acquired – few people would argue against driving tests or a qualification to practise surgery. Everything depends on how assessment is used, and the forms it takes. We need a better approach to assessment:

- We should reduce its prominence. It has become an obsession.
- We need to prevent it being used to exacerbate social inequalities. Low test scores should never result in learners being restricted to an unchallenging and monotonous curriculum.

● We have to guard against the backwash into teaching and learning, so that schools don't end up teaching to the test.

Paul Black and his colleagues at King's College London have demonstrated that *formative assessment* – helpful feedback rather than judgemental comment or grades – can have a positive impact on learning. Genuine feedback, such as a clear explanation of how to advance, is far more valuable to learners than marks or grades. This has brought about a major policy shift in Scotland, with the "Assessment is for Learning" initiative. Black's work is increasingly influential in England – although one key finding has been overlooked: if a teacher provides a mark or grade as well as verbal feedback, the feedback is ignored. [15]

There are better ways to recognise achievement than written tests. We don't check whether somebody can swim by getting them to write about it, so why do we rely so much on written tests in schools? A major development is under way in Queensland, Australia, using *rich tasks* instead of exams. [16]

A rich task is a performance or demonstration or product that is purposeful and models a life role. It presents substantive, real problems to solve and engages learners in forms of pragmatic social action that have real value in the world. The problems require identification, analysis and resolution, and require students to analyse, theorise and engage intellectually with the world. In this way, tasks connect to the world outside the classroom.

Rich tasks have to be valuable in themselves and not distract from real learning. They culminate in individual or team presentations, based on research and problem solving. They involve a range of skills, often connecting different subjects. The challenge must be meaningful to the learners – it could be set in a local context, with the results presented to an audience of parents or a community group.

If we really want to improve educational standards, we should use assessment that enhances learning rather than trivialising it. This could involve peer and self-assessment that is supportive rather than judgemental, and recognition for cooperative learning in groups rather than individual competitiveness. These forms of assessment would help to foster a genuine sense of learning community in our schools.

Rich Tasks

For 11 year olds

Multimedia Presentation of an Endangered Plant or Animal
Students will investigate a threatened plant or animal and the extent to which it is at risk. They will use this investigation to take constructive action and create a persuasive and informative multimedia presentation.

Oral Histories and Diverse and Changing Lifestyles
Students will explore change in, and diversity of, modern lifestyles, with particular reference to the nature of work, by recording oral histories from various members of their own community. These will form the basis for a media presentation that portrays changes in work practices in the past and predicts how they might change in the foreseeable future.

A Celebratory, Festive or Artistic Event or Performance
Students will work within teams, in different capacities, in planning, organising, creating and performing in a celebratory, festive or artistic event or performance that takes place at or outside the school.

For 16 year olds

Improving Health and Wellbeing in the Community
Students investigate the local situation through books, statistics and interviews, and acquire knowledge of some health issues, before presenting recommendations.

National Identity: Influences and Perspectives
This project involves the planning, production and presentation of a filmed documentary including information gleaned from research and interviews with people from different cultural backgrounds.

Opinion-Making Oracy
Students will make forceful speeches on an issue of international or national significance to different audiences.

The Shape We're In
Students investigate alternative shapes and/or dimensions for at least one container, a domestic object, a mechanical device and an object from nature. They then present an alternative design for one of these, explaining the maths.

CHAPTER 2

Full-spectrum surveillance

There are many positive ways to bring about widespread improvements in education. A classic example came in the 1970s when the school leaving age was raised from 15 to 16. Many teachers realised that they could not simply extend existing ways of learning by a year. The government commissioned an excellent series of television programmes showing examples of innovation and good practice, which were watched and discussed at staff meetings. There was no attempt to set a fixed blueprint, but money was made available to help schools implement their preferred ideas.

At around the same time the Schools Council, a government agency, promoted curriculum development through pilot studies involving volunteer schools. Resource packs and staff development materials were published and the new methods were made available for other teachers to adapt to their own schools.

In the 1970s and 1980s the Inner London Education Authority was a power house of curriculum development – until 1990, when the Tory government closed it down as dangerously progressive. It established teachers' centres where teachers met to write and publish resources that were used across the country.

Large-scale changes need a combination of factors to succeed. Creativity and cooperation are needed to produce and share good ideas. Teachers must be convinced that change is necessary. Schools and teachers need practical support and resources – especially time – to debate and think through the reform at grassroots level. Discussions have to involve the whole school community – staff, parents and students – in a genuine way. Teachers should not feel threatened or they will not dare take risks. Finally, there has to be enough freedom for each school to develop its own plan to suit local circumstances, priorities and interests. Most of these factors are absent in the present coercive regime.

The tide turned on school development in the 1980s under Thatcher, who seriously mistrusted teachers. Since then Labour and Conservative governments have pursued a highly centralised, top-down, negative and authoritarian model, with elaborate systems to control schooling in England. Directly and indirectly these systems govern every aspect of life in schools. This chapter shows the impact of this surveillance regime, how it came about, and how it might be challenged.[1]

High-stakes testing

"High-stakes testing" is the US term for tests that have serious and extended consequences beyond assessment itself. As the last chapter showed, tests are now used not just to give feedback to learners and recognise their knowledge, but to make far-reaching judgements about schools and teachers.

- Teachers' pay in England now depends partly on test scores, following the introduction of performance-related pay.
- Test and exam results heavily influence school inspections – the lead inspector studies test data even before the first visit to the school, then steers the team's judgements so they are consistent with the test scores.
- Test results are published in newspapers and crude comparisons are made between schools, regardless of the problems many pupils face in their lives.
- Parents are encouraged to use such crude comparisons as a basis for choosing schools.

Raising the stakes like this inevitably has a distorting effect on lessons, and the whole life of the school. Teachers start to focus on what the tests require, and to neglect other things that are important but cannot be tested. They coach pupils to write down the desired answers. Any attempt to dig deeper into a subject becomes a luxury. Teachers begin to feel guilty about teaching any topic that is not on the syllabus, or are put under pressure by anxious headteachers. Since it is easier to test the recall of simple factual information than more complex or controversial understanding, learning is systematically trivialised.

Recently there has been a shift from raw scores to "value-added" results, which take account of pupils' starting points. But this is not necessarily a fairer system: 11 to 16 year olds living in poverty tend to fall further behind, relative to the national average, due to all the extra problems in their lives, particularly during adolescence. Their test results may, therefore, show less "value added" than those of better off pupils. It is essential to recognise, though, that this is only a general trend – it is damaging to prejudge pupils' potential because of their background.

Whether inter-school comparisons are based on raw scores or value-added results, the consequence is that many teachers are frightened away from teaching in deprived neighbourhoods, as poor results could damage their future career prospects.

This high-stakes testing regime creates enormous pressure, but there are ways to challenge it through close analysis, ingenuity and solidarity. It is also evident that parents value other things besides test results. Challenging the power of testing requires the teaching profession to communicate well with parents, to build up trust and to form alliances. Schools need to communicate all the good things they achieve that are not reflected in test results. This can become a cynical public relations exercise if one school competes with another, but it can also be a means to challenge dominant attitudes to education and to highlight what is really valuable.

Inspection

Ofsted was set up in the early 1990s to increase the frequency of school inspections. Before Ofsted, schools were monitored by Her Majesty's Inspectorate of Education – the HMIs, who were highly respected for their experience and expertise. As well as giving advice to the schools they inspected, the HMIs used their visits partly to identify and share good practice and to suggest ways for other teachers to improve. These inspectors were well paid professionals in permanent posts.

Under Ofsted, a privatised system was established, with only 10 percent of England's HMIs remaining to carry out a few key functions.[2] Ofsted sub-contracts its inspection work to private profit-making companies. The cost is an enormous drain on spending but the price per inspection is quite low, since it uses a lot of part-time inspectors who are retired and drawing their pensions. Because they are on short-term contracts, often lasting three days at a time, the inspectors are unlikely to speak out critically about the impact of government policies on schools, however unhappy they are.

Ofsted's powers have been gradually extended to cover not just schools but also playgroups, teacher education and the work of education authorities. The consequences of failing an inspection have been heightened, leading to the privatisation of some education authorities as well as schools. Inspectors' decisions are not beyond challenge, though this is not easy.

We also need to recognise that Ofsted is not always fully in tune with government – it is formally a non-ministerial public body rather than a section of government, and has a degree of independence. Indeed Ofsted has sharply criticised the quality of teaching at two out of the first three city academies – the Business Academy, Bexley, and the Unity City Academy in Middlesbrough. Chief inspector David Bell's public pronouncements are sometimes "off message" as far as the government is concerned. Bell has, for example, opposed the narrow view of secondary education as vocational training. We can sometimes use inspectors' criticisms to expose poor policy.

Many teachers hoped that a Labour government would quickly wind down Ofsted, but it is now about to be strengthened. Labour's 2005 schools white paper, *Higher Standards, Better Schools for All*, promised to make inspection harsher, in order to close schools down and then privatise them.[3]

The National Curriculum

When Thatcher's ministers introduced the National Curriculum in 1988, they insisted that they intended to control what was taught but not how – this was to remain the teachers' prerogative. Labour's Tony Blair has changed all that. The National Curriculum is now supplemented by various "strategies" covering primary literacy and numeracy, primary schooling as a whole and key stage 3 (the lower years of secondary school). The strategies increasingly stretch across the whole curriculum.

They have not been uniformly bad – they include some good practice developed by innovative teachers, though presented without a clear philosophy – but they are particularly damaging when blindly and rigidly imposed. It is ironic that inspectors have blamed teachers for following official guidelines too closely.

The literacy strategy has been especially problematic. Though the literacy hour was not compulsory, schools were told they would be "interrogated" if they did not follow it and would have to prove the superiority of their alternative methods. This is difficult in practice, particularly for schools with lower test scores, although schools can use the mounting evidence and some very critical comments in official evaluations.

The National Curriculum, as first established, provided an outline of what should be taught by the end of each key stage – a period of two to four years. But the literacy strategy pinned down what should be taught every single term, however inappropriate for the age group or for particular pupils, and regardless of the class's interest.

Though the key stage 3 strategy contains many valuable ideas, these are undermined by a constant emphasis on the pace of learning. Everything is split into ten to 20-minute segments, making thoughtful learning next to impossible, while learners are encouraged to give brief but simplistic answers. Though group work does feature, the rigid structure of lessons and the rapid pace are an obstacle to genuine cooperation in problem-solving. The "starter activities" may make pupils more alert, but since they are generally unrelated to the main theme of the lesson, they do not help them to engage with it personally. Like the primary strategy, euphemistically called Excellence and Enjoyment, it is riddled with contradictions, and real enjoyment in learning is undermined by constant pressure.

A voice of experience

Shortly before retiring as Birmingham's director of education, Tim Brighouse denounced the government's overbearing control over education in England:

> Our national curriculum is more nationally prescriptive than any other state and is more so than the Stalinist regimes of the USSR.[4]

No one could write this off as the bitterness of an incompetent or disgruntled individual. Brighouse had just received a glowing report from Ofsted, declaring his leadership of Birmingham's local education authority as "outstanding... an energising and inspirational example...[showing] what can be done, even in the most demanding urban environments". His words reveal the deep discontent even among very respected senior figures. Brighouse also highlighted:

- the demoralising effect of key stage 2 SATs on many pupils, who are switched off education before secondary school

- the danger of tedious and repetitive remedial literacy programmes, and the need for experiences that will boost confidence and give a taste of success for those struggling with the "three Rs"
- the way performance pay sets teacher against teacher rather than encouraging them to learn from each other
- the competitive market system, which establishes "a self-perpetuating pecking order of schools" and "leaves a substantial minority...cast adrift"
- the government's "complete mistrust" of teachers, which cannot lead to real improvement because it damages morale and restricts creativity and initiative

It is worth noting that Scotland's educational standards are at least as good as England's, despite its more cautious use of testing, and not having Ofsted, performance pay for teachers or unbridled competition between schools. In chapter 4 we will see that Finland's education system, perhaps the highest performing in the world, is built on trusting teachers and their professional initiative rather than top-down control.

Re-shaping teachers and teaching

Performance pay was so strongly challenged by the unions that the Department for Education and Skills had to commission "research" to make it plausible. Commissioned from a private business rather than a university, the research used a methodology that was condemned as heavily flawed by a British Educational Research Association investigation.[5] The private research team had studied a sample of teachers identified by their headteachers as particularly good.

They found that only half taught in the approved way and only half had above average "value-added" results. The big problem was that the two halves didn't match. There was only a random connection between teaching in the approved manner and enhanced progress. Rather than rethink their assumptions, the researchers simply wrote off those teachers who did not fit the official mould, and based their recommendations for "effective" teaching on those who did.

Teaching is repeatedly being re-shaped on the basis of limited evidence but with a tacit assumption that teaching consists of the efficient transmission of knowledge. Much government policy seems to assume that children are empty jars into which teachers pour knowledge – and the faster they pour it, the more children will learn. This resembles the

model of teaching that Victorian novelist Charles Dickens satirised in *Hard Times*, rather than current views of learning as the social construction of understanding:

"Now, what I want is, Facts. Teach these boys and girls nothing but Facts. Facts alone are wanted in life. Plant nothing else, and root out everything else."

The speaker, and the schoolmaster all backed a little and swept with their eyes the inclined plane of little vessels then and there arranged in order, ready to have imperial gallons of facts poured into them until they were full to the brim.

Thomas Gradgrind, Sir. A man of realities. A man of facts and calculations. With a rule and a pair of scales, and the multiplication table always in his pocket, Sir, ready to weigh and measure any parcel of human nature, and tell you exactly what it comes to· He seemed a kind of cannon loaded to the muzzle with facts, and prepared to blow them clean out of the regions of childhood at one discharge. *Dickens, Hard Times*

A corrosive effect

Many writers have commented on the corrosive effect of the surveillance regime. It deeply affects teachers' motivation and relationships with learners, and produces lasting damage to schools as caring communities:

We feel like we have lost the closeness that we really value here... I feel ashamed really... Teachers are reporting a sense of despair at the scale of the demands they face...they are saying that they don't have time to build reasonable relationships with the students...they don't have the fun with students that they used to...give us the book and we'll teach is something I'm hearing more and more of but I know that it is a cry of despair... It is all so damn serious now, lots of suits, grey-suit reform. I feel compromised. (Headteachers interviewed by consultant Paul Clarke, 2001)

Michael Fielding, director of Sussex University's centre for innovation, asks:

How many teachers, particularly those of young children, are now able to listen openly, attentively, and in a non-instrumental, exploratory way to their children or students without feeling guilty, stressed or vaguely uncomfortable about the absence of criteria or the insistence of a target tugging at their sleeves.

London School of Economics Professor Richard Sennett has warned:

A regime that provides human beings with no deep reasons to care for one another cannot long preserve its legitimacy.

Canadian academics Coral Mitchell and Larry Sackney argue that poor relationships undermine the desire to really improve education:

Without trust, people divert their energy into self-protection and away from learning. When distrust pervades a school culture, it is unlikely that the school will be an energetic, motivating place.[6]

Accountability or responsibility?

These systems are supposed to increase "accountability", but Fred Inglis, one of the first writers to spot and condemn such managerialism in education, draws a sharp distinction:

Accountability is, after all, not the same thing as responsibility, still less duty. It is a pistol loaded with blame to be fired at the heads of those who cannot answer charges.[7]

Back in the 1980s Margaret Thatcher recognised that the public was no longer prepared to place blind trust in figures of authority, whether teachers, doctors or civil servants. She exploited this by creating a moral panic about supposedly low standards as a pretext for setting up new systems of surveillance. Thatcher relied on the rhetoric of accountability and a consumerist version of parental rights. In reality, teachers were made accountable not to parents but to the state. This did not lead to better dialogue with parents about their children's learning, but to a competitive scramble for places in particular schools.

Despite many good examples of cooperation between school and home, the teaching profession as a whole was vulnerable at that time because it had not worked closely enough with parents. Thatcher was able to take advantage of this. It is neither possible nor desirable to turn the clock back and insist on blind faith in professionals. But it is important to build a resistance to the phoney accountability of the present system by developing trust and openness.

There are many ways for teachers to cooperate with parents and give them information about their children's development. Education can only benefit from open dialogue between teachers, parents and students on aims and methods. The same applies to school evaluation. The data from test scores is limited and distorting, as are the judgements from an inspection system which is, in the last resort, punitive. John Macbeath, a pioneer of school self-evaluation, argues:

In healthy systems there is a sharing and networking of good practice within and among schools on a collegial basis. It is an unhealthy system which relies on the constant routine attentions of an external body to police its schools… In such a system there is an important role for an Inspectorate or Office of Standards: to make itself as redundant as possible.[8]

Macbeath helped to introduce a self-evaluation framework known as How Good Is Our School? to Scotland, and then to many other countries. Recently his work has focused on involving learners in the evaluation and improvement of their schools – the "student voice" project. One approach, developed in Austria, has been to give children cameras. Their photographs are mounted on posters as the basis for discussion. This has helped to overcome the imbalance of power when adults interview children. It revealed that children have very different experiences of school than teachers, and has led to genuine improvements.

School self-evaluation can be a powerful way of bringing about real improvement. Often schools invite in teachers from other schools as "critical friends", to see things with different eyes and help them avoid complacency. But this is undermined, however, because it is being introduced into England's punitive system. It has become a burden for headteachers, requiring massive extra work – almost doing the inspectors' job for them – while becoming yet another thing for Ofsted to check up on. Now "school improvement partners" are being imposed on schools. This is a characteristic perversion of the critical friend concept. They will be used punitively, including as a means to close and privatise schools, and commercial agencies will undoubtedly be asked to market this service.

Some projects for student involvement are much more radical. A team of Black and Hispanic lecturers at the University of California's Cesar Chavez Institute set up a summer school for disaffected young people. These 17 and 18 year olds went out to interview school management. Some were outraged when principals threatened to throw them off the premises for asking inconvenient questions, but they insisted on their right as researchers. The students made a video to expose school conditions, such as a heavy police presence, and a curriculum that did not deal with neighbourhood problems. The video finishes with extracts from patronising reading books that the State of California has imposed on the weakest 25 percent of readers, exposing the gap between these texts and the students' real lives.[9]

Evaluation need not be authoritarian. It does not need to be based on data that distorts. The word "evaluation" should remind us that judgements depend on values, rather than supposedly value-free statistics. It is not a neutral process. We have to decide whether our judgements are based on the immorality and amorality of neo-liberalism or on progressive and democratic values. Enlightened evaluation challenges poor provision, especially for the most vulnerable young people. It can unearth the evidence to challenge inequality and superficiality. Instead of the present "name and shame" culture, teachers and schools need constructive criticism and a supportive climate for change.

CHAPTER 3

Improving schools
– or speeding up the conveyor belt?

There are many ways to improve schools and enhance achievement. In Finland the priority has been to make sure that all pupils are well nourished – free healthy meals for every child. Teachers are highly motivated and constantly reviewing how they teach. Finnish politicians do not "name and shame" schools, and teaching is a popular career choice. According to the OECD's international tests, Finland now has the most successful education system in the world.[1]

My own interest in school improvement began around 1995, when I visited a school on a very poor council estate in Rochdale, Greater Manchester, where GCSE results had dramatically improved.[2] They had risen from 7 percent of pupils gaining five or more A to C grades to 47 percent, over four years, without any statistical trickery. At the start of this period the school had almost closed – only 60 students had entered its Year 7, with many lost to neighbouring schools.

An inspired headteacher and staff had made many changes, few of which accorded with orthodox ideas about improving schools. They had a mural painted the full height of a tall ugly chimney at the school entrance. The head and deputies moved out of their offices into a large empty classroom, removing the door so that they could be fully available. They discouraged students from going off site at lunchtime by providing lots of social and leisure facilities. Assemblies became confidence-building events, full of drama, dance, quizzes, talent contests.

During my visit I watched a cleaner coaching students through their dance steps for the next day. A well liked form tutor was released from some of her normal teaching to follow her class from subject to subject and help coach them towards higher grades. One way of raising boys' achievement was to counter traditional macho attitudes, including encouraging many into the GCSE childcare option.

Inspiring examples of school improvement in working class areas have been based on a genuine empowerment. The title of my first book, *The Power to Learn*, emerged during an interview with a primary school head in a very poor district of Manchester. She told me about the ten year olds running computer courses for their teachers and for parents. The book is full of stories of creative and courageous teachers helping inner city pupils to achieve remarkable levels of success. The teachers and heads were driven by a commitment to the children and families, a belief in social justice and the desire to encourage young people's concern about social and political issues.[3] Sadly these are not the principles driving official school improvement under New Labour, with its insistence on quality control and "effectiveness".

We should beware of taking government rhetoric about school improvement at face value. One of the problems with phrases such as *effective teaching* and *school improvement* is that nobody feels they can disagree. It's like being asked whether you're in favour of personal hygiene or being kind to animals.

The government's constant repetition of the words *effective* and *improving* is deeply ideological – it suggests these are simply commonsense concepts that are unambiguous, shared and universally valid. In fact, they help to create a new "common sense" of false assumptions about education. The constant repetition of buzzwords such as *excellence, standards* and *choice* hide reactionary programmes behind positive rhetoric.

Before you set about improving schools, you need to work out what would count as a good school. That depends on your view of society, your aspirations for young people and your hope for the future. How we change schools depends on how we want to change the world.[4]

School Effectiveness

In the 1960s a major US government report used statistics to show the continuing injustice and inequality of educational provision for Black Americans.[5] It showed that differences in educational attainment correlated strongly with objective factors such as different levels of funding, teacher qualifications and so on, as well as with family differences – parents' education, books in the home and poverty. For the US at the time, it was a groundbreaking report challenging poverty and institutional racism. It exposed the enduring inequalities despite the gains of the civil rights movement.

School Effectiveness research supplied a counter-attack to this new sociology. Its researchers discovered some differences between schools even after poverty factors were taken into account – a difference in schools' "effectiveness", or a "school effect". School Effectiveness research preferred to focus on what teachers and school leaders could do to "make a difference". Separating off social deprivation and focusing on teachers and heads was an ideological choice, as these words from two of its leading proponents show:

> Pragmatists, working within the SER [School Effectiveness Research] paradigm, believe that efforts to alter the existing relationship between social class and student achievement by bringing about broad societal changes are *naive, perhaps quixotic*. We prefer to *work within the constraints of the current social order.*[6]

While recognising that schools and teachers including good leadership and management do make a difference, exaggerating the impact can lead to a blame culture:

Teachers who have dared to mention the subject have been branded defeatist or patronising for even considering that social background can make a difference... Schools with high proportions of disadvantaged pupils need extra support. Teachers who choose to work in these schools need their commitment recognised and supported.[7]

School Effectiveness, which conveniently emphasises the "effectiveness" of schools and sidelines social and economic factors, has become dominant, thanks to considerable government support and sponsorship. It has also been spread internationally, through agencies such as the OECD and the World Bank, but is nowhere stronger than in England.

The ideology of School Effectiveness research
There are many problems with School Effectiveness research:

- It avoids a debate about the purposes of education. What do we really value most in a good school? Is it quadratic equations or environmental understanding, creativity, or spelling? These are political and philosophical questions that are not solved by comparing test scores.
- School Effectiveness regards the social context of the school as a mere background factor – but in real schools teachers and heads need to engage creatively with the experiences and aspirations of the local community, especially in poor neighbourhoods.
- Since School Effectiveness uses statistical methods, it must focus on "outputs" that are easy to quantify. Consequently, it emphasises exam and test results to the neglect of all the other aims of education. It has helped create the climate where the only things that matter are those you can measure. And a correlation between two factors does not prove cause and effect. Sometimes two factors are only accidentally connected, or act reciprocally. For example, good attendance makes teaching more successful – but equally, inspiring teachers can lead to better attendance.
- Emphasising the "school effect" avoids the kind of sociological determinism that says, "There is nothing we can do – it's down to the pupils' background." But instead it sows the illusion that poverty can be overcome by schools alone, without a wider political struggle. We end up with a modern version of the Victorian ideology of the "self-made man", satirised by Dickens in *Hard Times*:

Any capitalist there, who had made sixty thousand pounds out of sixpence, always professed to wonder why the sixty thousand nearest Hands didn't each make sixty thousands pounds out of sixpence, and more or less reproached them everyone for not accomplishing the little feat. What I did you can do. Why don't you go and do it?

Misleading claims

The School Effectiveness model is now the framework for statistical comparisons made by the government and the Ofsted school inspectorate. But it is important to understand how these comparisons can be misleading, despite claims that they are "fair".

Comparisons are now based less on raw test results and more on a "value-added" approach – one that measures children's progress compared with their level of attainment a few years earlier. This sounds plausible but can be misleading because the attainment gap linked to socioeconomic factors is greater during adolescence than at primary school age. This means that secondary schools in the poorest neighbourhoods tend to make less progress compared with the national average, and so show less "value added".

Other statistics are said to be fair because they compare "similar schools". The schools are usually grouped together based on the percentage of pupils entitled to free school meals. But this is a crude indicator that does not say anything about the rest of the school population. School A and School B might each have 25 percent of pupils entitled to free meals, but in School A another 25 percent of pupils have parents who are university graduates in professional occupations, while in School B there are none. It is unfair to blame School B if fewer pupils gain high grades.[8]

School Effectiveness research not only calculates the differences between schools, but also claims to identify the factors that make a difference. Such research has produced a series of bland statements:

- strong positive leadership by the head and senior staff
- a clear and continuing focus on teaching and learning
- well-developed procedures for assessing how pupils are progressing
- rewards and incentives to encourage pupils to success

These features might appear at first sight to be magic bullets that only need to be fired in order to make a school more effective. On closer scrutiny, they are confusing:

- "Strong leadership" can mean anything from supportive and inspirational to dictatorial.
- A "focus on teaching and learning" is equally vague, and might simply reinforce poor practice.
- Assessment does not necessarily improve progress, and some uses of assessment are demoralising.
- There is also a world of difference between relying on school rewards, such as gold stars and merit certificates, and emphasising the intrinsic rewards of learning, for example by encouraging students to be proud of their work through regular displays and performances, or working in teams to solve problems.

Alternative messages from the statistics

Fortunately some statistical studies take a broader approach. David Gillborn and his colleagues at London University's Institute of Education have exposed the links between school attainment and race and class.[9] They have also been able to demonstrate that low achievement is not inevitable. African-Caribbean pupils are not below average when they start school and receive lots of parental support. Why are they the least successful group by age 16? In at least one local education authority area this is not the case, and African-Caribbean pupils are the highest achievers – so low achievement is not inevitable.

School Effectiveness studies in Latin America use some of the statistical techniques of researchers in the US and England, but often show a more genuine concern with overcoming poverty. European research has begun to show how the link between school achievement and social circumstances varies between different countries, according to their politics and social priorities. Recent OECD international studies have examined carefully the correlation between family background and attainment in different countries.[10] They show:

- a very weak link in Finland, where all pupils receive a healthy free meal at school
- that being brought up by a single parent makes no difference to school success in Austria, at one extreme, and a massive difference in the US with its minimal welfare provision
- the correlation between attainment and family background is very high in Germany because pupils are segregated into different levels of school at the age of ten and this drags down attainment levels overall

The international researchers insist there is no contradiction between quality and equality, between excellence and social justice. German analysis of the research notes:

> The achievement of the highest socioeconomic groups is very similar in different countries, but the achievement of the lowest groups is radically different. The highest achieving countries have the smallest spread. The way to raise standards overall is to concentrate on raising the achievement of the poorest sections of society.[11]

The countries with the highest achievement are generally those that have reduced poverty, but also reduced its impact on educational success. To really raise a country's educational standards overall, efforts should be concentrated not just on educating the poorest children but on eliminating child poverty.

School Improvement

Partly in reaction to the limitations of School Effectiveness, a body of writing known as School Improvement has emerged, connected to a growth industry of consultancies to support change. Ideological factors are at work here too.

School Improvement concentrates on the processes needed to bring about change. It relies on a close qualitative study rather than statistical data – interviewing teachers and visiting schools.

School Improvement has brought considerable insights into how to promote change, which is important. In principle at least, it stresses cooperative involvement and participation rather than autocratic management, and the importance of involving the whole school community – staff, parents, students. Without a clear sense of social purpose however, collegiality and cooperation can mean complicity in change for the worse.

Unfortunately School Improvement tends to accept without question the outcomes of schooling that are overemphasised by School Effectiveness researchers and the government – test results.

This is not to suggest that exam results are unimportant. Indeed, if you live in the wrong part of town or your skin is the wrong colour, you need your certificates more than anybody – but they are never enough. It takes a lot more to see you through. And schools are unlikely to improve the exam results of the poorest students by piling on the pressure.

As with School Effectiveness, writers on School Improvement in England – not only in academic books but in mountains of official documents and advice – are virtually silent about the purpose of schooling. Leaving the direction of change off the agenda leads readers to accept as self-evident that the main purpose of educational change is to notch up test scores. Everything else is just a means to this end. This gives rise to some very strange writing. Dozens of books are published every year about styles of leadership but few even consider where they are leading to.

School Improvement uses words such as "vision" and "values" in an ethereal way, emptied of meaning. Often "vision" means little more than minor organisational changes. This is like rearranging the deckchairs on the *Titanic*. "Values" appear in the context of "valuing good behaviour" or "placing a high value on examination results" rather than social or political values. None of this relates to the big changes taking place in the world, or to our hopes for the future, which should determine the direction of educational change.

This way of talking about school improvement and leadership strengthens neo-liberal ideology. By keeping silent about human values, it reinforces a sense that monetary values are all that matters – the bottom line. By failing to discuss alternative futures, it reinforces the sense of inevitability and fatalism that neo-liberal politicians use to quell dissent:

> The neo-liberal version of the performing school requires teachers and students to be followers, but to feel good about it… Teachers talk about "pseudo-participation" where views are sought as a ritual rather than a sincere attempt to listen and take note… The problems of the education system have been laid at the door of teachers while their capacity for finding solutions has been taken away. The rhetoric has been of empowerment, participation and teams, but the reality is that teachers have had to continue to do what they have always done – be empowered to do what they have been told to do. **Helen Gunter**

Not surprisingly, teachers often become cynical when asked to participate – even when the proposed change is genuinely beneficial. What is missing is the power and freedom to look at the changing world, build a vision of the future we would like and design a school to help take us there.[12]

Leadership and change management are not entirely empty concepts. An inspired individual who really knows how to work with others can help to transform a school, but this depends as much on deeply held social and educational values as on management techniques. I quote from two Glasgow headteachers whose own background has affected the way they have changed their schools:

> I get very angry when people write off working class communities, partly because that's the background I'm from. My parents were keen that all of us gained qualifications, and it upsets me to hear people talk as if parents in an area don't care about education.
> **Carol Howarth, who helped to reconnect her primary school with the local community and involved children democratically in running it.**

> We have had [asylum seeker] families removed in the middle of the night to the detention centre at Dungavel, people who suffered terribly in their home countries. But we should also question the words economic migrant. My own family were economic migrants from Ireland. It's about survival, not greed, and a natural desire for a decent life. And many Scots left for the US and Canada as economic migrants.
> **Tom MacDonald, who helped make his secondary school a safe haven and a place of opportunity for asylum seekers.**[13]

Poverty and racism: turning schools around

Mainstream writers on school improvement are slowly waking up to the challenge of poverty and racism – and about time. Very little has been written about what enhances school success in the most deprived neighbourhoods. A key piece of research on successful schooling for African-Caribbean pupils[14] highlighted several important factors:

- a strong and determined lead on equal opportunities from the headteacher
- schools listened to and learned from pupils and their parents and tried to see things from the student's point of view
- schools created careful links with local communities
- schools tried to understand the "whole child" – there were close links between children's welfare and their academic interests and needs
- commonly perceived setbacks such as a poor command of English were seen as challenges to be met, rather than excuses for underachievement
- they had clear procedures for responding to racist bullying and harassment
- there were clear systems for targeting, tracking and monitoring individual student progress

This is a very different set of priorities to the normal "characteristics of effective schools". It is important to step beyond managerialism and pay full attention to the curriculum, teaching and learning, ethos and relationships and links with parents and the community.[15]

A deep and sustainable reform of schools cannot be achieved without political struggle. Teachers and parents committed to social justice and a real education have to engage in a struggle both within and beyond the school. Even the basic catchphrases of school improvement need to be rethought. "Raising expectations" is a political as well as psychological issue – it has to be about the expectations of the whole community, not only improving opportunities for a few. This defies the logic of capitalism, which dictates that some people are worth less than others.

"Turning a school around" involves turning it to engage with the community and transforming the school's values and ambitions in favour of social justice and equality. Genuine school leadership is more than a technical skill – it is first and foremost a social commitment, a determination to work for a better future.

Finally, as in the past, it also requires a collective struggle from teacher unions and support from parents for more teachers and smaller classes. There is currently a lot of government rhetoric about 'personalised learning' but no political will to make classes small enough for teachers to really respond to their students as diverse and active individuals.

CHAPTER 4

Dividing communities
– privatising schools

My 80 year old mother never tires of saying how glad she is that her children had a good education. She remembers the day when hers came to a halt. She had sat the first part of the Scholarship (the entrance exam for grammar school, later known as the 11-plus), scoring the highest in her class. The head then told her there was no point in her sitting the final part because her family couldn't afford the grammar school uniform. Like most of her class she stayed at elementary school till she started work at 14. She soon stopped reading at school – she had read every book in the cupboard and couldn't stomach the teacher's advice to start all over again.

Working class parents are constantly being blamed for their low expectations and are frequently described by sociologists as "culturally deprived". We should learn from history – it has been a long and active process of deprivation.

A long struggle took place through the middle of the 20th century for comprehensive secondary schools which are open to all. An uneasy compromise was reached at the end of World War II, when three types of secondary school were established, supposedly "separate but equal". They were supposed to meet the needs of three different kinds of learner. There were grammar schools for "academic children", technical high schools for children with "good brains" but more technical interests – although these were never actually established in many areas – and secondary modern schools for the rest.

To get into grammar or technical schools, 10 year olds had to pass the 11-plus, including a strange test of abstract logic. This was supposedly a test of natural intelligence, but practice could significantly improve scores.

These schools reflected not different types of brain, but three sections of society. The secondary moderns – a euphemism – provided a low-status and limited curriculum, minimally qualified teachers, meagre resources and a tough disciplinary environment, chiefly for manual working class children. Secondary modern schooling was a cul-de-sac leading to few qualifications or prospects.

Gradually the flaws became apparent. Some children, consigned to the secondary modern school as 11-plus failures, took the O level exam intended for the grammar school pupils and passed. The argument was eventually won for comprehensive secondary schools for all pupils – a system implemented right across Scotland and Wales, but only piecemeal in England.

As well as greater equality and social cohesion, comprehensive education led to a massive rise in standards – a fact that nostalgic Conservatives and modernising Blairites prefer to forget. In 1960 when around 20 percent of children were selected for grammar schools, only 16 percent of 16 year olds achieved five O level passes. In 2000 – in a system which was still largely comprehensive despite erosion by market competition – over 50 percent achieved the equivalent five A to C grades at GCSE. In 1970, 47 percent of children left school with no qualifications at all, but by 1999 only 10 percent did so.

In 1963 the Robbins Report on higher education, commissioned by the then Conservative government, set a target that 17 percent of young people should enter university. By 2000 34 percent did so, with an even higher percentage in Scotland. This certainly does not support government claims that comprehensive schools are a failure.[1]

Comprehensive education didn't solve every problem, of course, and social inequalities continued to have a more complex influence on achievement. Some of the new schools were too large, and some were internally divided into streams and "ability bands", but the reform provided a foundation for future development. The ongoing attack on comprehensive schools is clearly not for educational reasons.

The international evidence: Finland's comprehensive system

In the OECD's international study of 15 year olds in 2000, Finland came highest in literacy, fourth in maths, and third in science out of 32 countries. Many people were surprised at this, not least the Finns.[2]

Finnish researchers pointed first of all to high levels of equality and a universal system of comprehensive schools. Finland had hardly any low-scoring students. As well as having relatively little poverty, Finland works hard to limit the effect of family background on children's education. The international study showed that the impact of parental background is about twice as strong in Britain, one of the most extreme cases.

There is little variation between schools in different communities, which the research team put down to the comprehensive school system. Only 5 percent of Finnish schools scored below the international average. This isn't only because of schools, but the entire system of youth provision. The researchers state:

> Providing all students with equal educational opportunities and removing obstacles to learning especially among the least successful students have been leading principles in Finnish education policy.

The researchers note that in Finland:
- All pupils receive healthy school meals completely free of charge.
- With an excellent network of libraries, 44 percent of Finland's 15 year olds borrow books at least once a month, almost double the

international average. Three out of four spend some time reading for enjoyment each day.

- Teachers are well qualified, each with a masters degree, and with substantial staff development based on teachers carrying out research into teaching and learning.
- Teachers are very highly regarded and there is strong competition to enter teaching degree courses. Teachers are trusted and there is no system of inspection.
- There is a good school health service, and students with special needs receive social, psychological and educational support.
- The curriculum has a common core, but is also flexible and designed to meet individual interests. Projects and investigations are frequent. Engagement and enjoyment, as well as learning strategies, are the key.
- Pupils are not put into "sets" at school – there is a good tradition of mixed-ability teaching and small classes.
- Teachers demonstrate good learning strategies rather than putting on pressure.
- Assessment is not based on end of year tests and there is no exam at the end of compulsory schooling, but teachers provide regular feedback to students and their families.

Altogether the Finnish system ensures that social background makes very little difference.

Germany's selective system

There are some comprehensive schools in Germany, but these are attended by only 9 percent of students. Even these are usually in competition with grammar schools in the same town, losing high-flying pupils. Most children are placed in one of three levels of school, the lowest containing mainly children of unskilled or unemployed workers and migrant families.

A deep sense of shock went through Germany when the international data from the OECD study was published. The German researchers exposed the social injustice and waste of talent in this system, and its consequence – low results overall.[3] Even when pupils had identical attainment in reading, the children of "upper professional" parents were three times as likely to get into grammar school as the children of skilled manual occupations. The divided system results in a high proportion of students at the lowest levels in reading, maths and science – and the grammar schools don't even compensate by producing above average numbers of high achievers.

It is often argued that raising standards can only be achieved if we stop worrying about social differences. The OECD data shows the very opposite. It defies all logic that Blair's government says comprehensive schools have had their day and is seeking to re-establish a divided system of education by all kinds of devious means.

Eroding the comprehensive school system

In the 1980s Margaret Thatcher's Tory government attempted to re-divide some English comprehensive schools into grammars and secondary moderns. This was actively resisted by parents – especially those who realised that siblings would be sent to separate schools. Ever since, Conservative and New Labour governments have been trying to destroy the comprehensive system by stealth in England. In Scotland all state-funded secondary schools are comprehensive and this is rarely questioned.

League tables were introduced to encourage parents to make an active choice of secondary school. Since the higher scoring schools tend to be in the richer suburbs, with more advantaged students, this also led more ambitious working class families to abandon the local schools, hoping that their children might do better elsewhere. This caused a downward spiral for many inner city or council estate schools. They were left with vacancies, which were then filled by pupils expelled by other schools as too troublesome or difficult to teach. Some schools with empty places found it difficult to balance the books, since they had to keep their buildings in decent repair on a restricted budget.

This policy was promoted as "parental choice", but often means schools choosing parents, not parents choosing schools.[4] Competition is particularly fierce in London and entry to many schools depends on having parents who know how to play the game.

Various kinds of schools have been set up to attract more affluent or better educated parents. Specialist schools are now allowed to select a percentage of pupils on the basis of "aptitude". Since it is hard to demonstrate the potential of a ten year old to learn Chinese or business, this usually means better opportunities for those whose parents can exert influence. In other cases, "aptitude" means having parents who can afford piano lessons or home computers. It is important to acknowledge teacher resistance, however – most specialist schools have refused to select pupils in this way.

Some schools now interview prospective parents to check the family's suitability.[5] Prospective pupils are asked questions such as, "What do you do when you get home from school?" One successful candidate informed me that he'd told the headteacher he went to his room to read a book or work at his computer. In fact, he normally played football with his friends – but a more honest friend didn't get into the school.

Many parents are devoting enormous effort to making sure their children get into the "right school". They have been turned into consumers of education rather than partners. Research by Cambridge University professor Diane Reay has found some parents spending over £100 a week on private tuition, music and drama lessons – more than some single mothers get in benefits to live on.[6] The system discriminates against manual or unemployed workers and many ethnic groups.

Racial segregation is another serious consequence of parental choice in this quasi-market. Many white parents have cynically resorted to attending church when their children reach the age of nine or ten, to gain a ticket to their preferred secondary school – often the one with fewest Muslim pupils. Given the dangers of educational apartheid and the attack on Muslim communities following the London bombs of July 2005, Blair's support for church schools is a real problem.

Obviously, while there are Anglican and Catholic schools, other religions have a right to theirs – but it is time for us to discuss as a society whether religious segregation of schools aids the development of a multi-ethnic society. We should be looking at how the positive values held by particular religions and cultures can be discussed and shared with others.

... finally destroying it

When he introduced the (2005) White Paper, Blair promised that it would bring about "irreversible" change. He was right. If it was carried into legislation and action, it would probably mean the end of the comprehensive school system. The White Paper wanted every school (primary as well as secondary) to become a "trust school", each with the power to set its own admissions policy. In other words, it could choose which pupils to allow in and whose children to turn away.

This was an audacious move, but the Prime Minister overplayed his hand and faced a massive revolt among his own MPs. He had to retreat, but the danger remains that when enough schools are privatised as trust schools, they will simply do what they like. It will not be long before full-blown selection at 11 becomes the norm if Blair's reforms come into force. In fact, the forms of selection already used in many English city schools are more blatant forms of discrimination than the 11 plus exam was.

At the time of writing, the Education and Inspections Bill is being debated in parliament. The bill has also quietly introduced a new route to a divided education – dividing pupils from age 14 into either an academic or a vocational track. The bill says pupils choosing a vocational diploma will have no entitlement to study history or geography, a language, design and technology or creative and performing arts – music, dance, drama or art. For pupils in the vocational stream, even English lessons will be stripped of literature, personal writing and media studies when an alternative "functional English" is introduced.

The division, once established, will soon shift backwards into the lower secondary years. The proposed new system is quite different to the comprehensive schools of the 1970s and 1980s, when nobody suggested that opting for car mechanics or childcare should prevent a student from also studying history or drama.[7]

Privatisation and the attack on comprehensive education

Private finance has traditionally had quite a minor role in schools – providing separate elite private schools for those who can afford the fees. But in the last ten to 20 years publicly funded education has become a milk cow for commercial profiteering.

When school meals became a profit-making business, this had disastrous consequences for children's health. The supply of computers is big business, and exaggerated claims flow from government offices about the value of IT for children's learning.

Local councils used to pay for new buildings through loans – now construction companies and banks build and own new buildings, leasing them back for profit through the private finance initiative (PFI) or other forms of public-private partnership (PPP). A survey by the main Scottish teachers' union, EIS, found:

- classrooms that were too small for active learning, and would only accommodate a class provided it is seated permanently in rows
- schools tied in to computer maintenance contracts, and experiencing long delays before repairs are carried out
- inadequate ventilation, so teachers and students became sleepy
- minimal standards of insulation, leading to high heating bills and environmental damage
- schools that had been rebuilt without a staffroom, leaving teachers of different subjects without a space to talk to each other
- instances where teachers were forbidden to display pupils' work on the walls – these "belong to the company" and teachers were "only entitled to the space between them"
- cases where the private owners had gone bankrupt and sold the schools on – in one education authority, school buildings are now owned and run by a Spanish railway company[8]

Blair's government is now taking the final step in privatising state schools, as academies and trust schools. Now it is not just the building that will be privately owned, but the school itself will be privately managed.

The academies: stealing our schools

How would you like your local school to be run by a second hand car dealer? New Labour's latest scheme for inner city regeneration, the creation of "city academies", means precisely that. Two academies are now controlled by fundamentalist Christian car dealership millionaire Sir Peter Vardy. City academies are run under the control of businesses or religious organisations. Any company executive with £2 million to spare can become the proud owner of your local school as its "sponsor". The latest offer, it appears, is three schools for the price of two, with perhaps a peerage thrown in...

The academies programme is a wonderful bargain for the business sponsor. The government puts up most of the cash for a new school building – around £30 million – from our taxes, which also pay all the running costs. But in this unique business arrangement the public does not have a single "share" in the "business". The school – including its staff and curriculum – is under the control of the business sponsors. Without any democratic accountability, the sponsor appoints the governing body. They appoint the head. They choose the teachers. They even decide what children will learn.

Christian fundamentalists like Vardy have shown massive interest. There are now state-funded schools – including the two academies sponsored by Vardy – that expect pupils to believe that god created the world in six days, denying Darwin's theory of evolution.

Sponsors can recoup large amounts of their initial £2 million stake by selling off part of the school grounds as building land. One school passed back £300,000 to the sponsor's family for "services rendered" – according to researchers from the BBC's *File on 4*, more than £100,000 was handed over for advertising and recruitment advice alone. A recent *Guardian* report revealed that very little of the sponsorship money had actually been handed over.[9]

This is asset stripping on a massive scale. The government's plan is to create 200 academies in inner cities and other poor urban areas by 2010 – private companies will own nearly half of all schools in poor areas.

The scheme is asset stripping in another sense too – a bid to control minds. Nobody can be sure where business involvement in schools might lead. In the US hundreds of thousands of teenagers are forced to watch one commercial TV channel for 20 minutes a day – not an educational programme but adverts and the channel's version of the news – just because it provides the school with equipment. Most academies here specialise in business, enterprise or computing. Notoriously, pupils at The Business Academy, Bexley, spend their Fridays doing business and stock exchange simulations and other training. A mini stock exchange stands in the school foyer.

Do the academies work?

New Labour claims to be the champion of the poor. Labour insists on schools overcoming the effects of poverty – but it is not so desperate as to eliminate child poverty itself. The city academies are the latest magic cure. First, the government claims the academy programme is a way of getting money to rebuild run down inner city schools – a strange argument since more than 90 percent of the funding comes from our taxes. The small amount contributed by sponsors does not justify the loss of public and professional control.

Labour also argues that the academies are more successful. This flies in the face of the evidence so far. Of the first three academies to open, in 2002, two had worse GCSE results in 2004 than their predecessor schools did in 2001.[10] The third was found by inspectors to have serious weaknesses in teaching. One of the first three was failed by Ofsted inspectors and put into "special measures".

Blair's education ministers insist that the city academies are improving three times as fast as non-academy schools and use this to justify moves to hand over many other schools to trusts led by businesses or faith groups. But closer examination of the data shows that this is almost entirely due to a shift from GCSE courses to GNVQs that could be counted as "equivalent" to four higher grade GCSEs – the manoeuvre detailed in Chapter 1.[11]

After the 2004 exam results were published, the government was forced to introduce a new measure of schools' achievement, counting the pupils who gained five or more good GCSEs "or equivalents" only when their results included GCSEs in both English and maths. Calculations under this new official system show that the city academies have improved only marginally on the performance of their predecessor schools. The proportion of pupils hitting the new benchmark increased only from 14.3 percent to 14.9 percent with the introduction of the academies – a figure that actually represents just three pupils across 11 city academies. [12]

The academies, supposedly serving the most deprived areas, have also begun to expel less successful pupils. The two academies in Middlesbrough have expelled 61 pupils in two years – compared with just 15 expelled by the other seven Middlesbrough schools. That is certainly one way to improve your percentage scores. At West London Academy, with a total of 746 students, there were 265 fixed-term and 20 permanent exclusions.

Hundreds of concerned parents of pupils at the new Trinity Academy in Doncaster, South Yorkshire, turned up to voice their anger at the school's strict discipline. This can be a way of shifting the population, by encouraging local parents to take their children elsewhere.

Other elements of the academy school system have a similar effect. To get into the Mossbourne Academy in the east London borough of Hackney, pupils have to sit hours of tests. This is supposedly a way of ensuring a balanced intake, but it is social selection – it ensures that only the most determined and well organised families get their children in.

Sometimes the claims of the academies and their sponsors to be serving deprived neighbourhoods can be exposed by looking at free school meal statistics. Lambeth Academy, south London, opened with 9 percent of its pupils receiving free school meals. But the average across the borough is 40 percent and one Lambeth school has 85 percent of pupils on free meals.

Of course not all academies are poor. Some might show creativity in rethinking the curriculum or school organisation. Some academy headteachers appear determined to open their doors to all local children. The problem is not individual cases but an insane government policy that invites injustice and abuse. There are many other ways to support creativity and innovation without handing schools over to private businesses.

Where are the academies going?

This is a massive project, dreamed up by New Labour spin-merchants with precious little evidence or research behind it. Education authorities are being bludgeoned into line with threats that they will get no other money for new buildings. Where there is a shortage of schools, they are told that academies are the only answer. Where schools have become run down and demoralised, control by private business sponsors is presented as the panacea, rather than democratic local support and the development of a community school which truly serves the neighbourhood.

It is still unclear – perhaps even to the government – where the city academies strategy is leading. There are various possibilities, but the academies clearly serve a number of New Labour aims for education:

- The academies are potentially another route to reintroduce selection at 11. Surrounding schools will find it difficult to compete with the sparkling new academy and its hi-tech façade. Academies will find ingenious ways to choose or turn away new pupils.
- Most of the academies have a business, enterprise or IT specialism. Academies are not required to follow the National Curriculum. It is increasingly clear that the government wishes to replace a broad curriculum with preparation for work for many young people, and is openly proposing "specialist vocational schools". The academies can serve as a flagship to tie education closely to employers' requirements from age 11 rather than meeting the broad educational needs of young people and a democratic society.
- This new model of publicly funded but privately owned schools can be extended beyond inner city areas. Indeed, the 2006 Education and Inspections Bill does precisely that.

But businesses are not exactly rushing forward to take direct control of schools, in an echo of what happened to the Conservatives' failed City Technology Colleges policy. More secure profits can be made by selling school meals, or through the privatisation of buildings and computer systems. Many businesses prefer to set the schools agenda indirectly (see Chapter 8). The academies policy has also angered a number of New Labour MPs, and the House of Commons Education and Skills Select Committee was very critical of it.

Several academies have already been stopped by parents and the campaign is growing. In Conisbrough, South Yorkshire, teachers and parents forced Christian fundamentalist Vardy to withdraw his sponsorship of a proposed academy. Their protests included offering the school for sale on the internet auction website eBay and running a mock car sale in the playground. The slogan in this former mining community was: "They've taken the pits and taken our jobs – they're not getting our schools."

In Walthamstow, east London, fashion designer Jasper Conran abandoned plans to sponsor an academy after a revolt by parents and pupils at the school it would have replaced. Islington Green School, in north London, has beaten off one takeover bid. In Lambeth, south London, a proposal that would have closed a popular primary school was defeated. In all these cases, the academies have been fought off through a vigorous campaign uniting staff and parents and sometimes the students themselves.

We urgently need to build up this popular resistance. Parents and activists in the teaching unions are building a campaign at grassroots level – a dynamic alliance of students, parents and staff – with Birmingham NUT serving as the organising centre.

More privatisation: the move towards "trust schools"
It now turns out that the disastrous academies policy is only the tip of the iceberg. The government's 2005 education white paper, *Higher Standards,*

Better Schools for All proposed to extend privatisation and autonomy. It proposed that every school, primary as well as secondary, should become a "trust school" – or "independent state school" – with the power to set its own admissions policy and choose which pupils to allow in and whose children to turn away.

This was an audacious move, but the prime minister overplayed his hand and faced a massive revolt among his own Labour MPs. When the 2006 Education and Inspections Bill based on the white paper was published, ministers were forced to retreat and concede that schools would not be compelled to take on trust status. But the danger remains that when enough schools are privatised as trust schools, they will simply do what they like.

The proposed trust schools will be funded by our taxes but will not be controlled by the public in any way, whether through local education authority representatives or through elected staff and parent representatives on governing bodies. They will be run by "trusts" set up by businessmen or "faith groups". The trusts will choose their own governing body. Each trust school will be a law unto itself and the termination of local authority control will provide carte blanche for all kinds of corruption.

The trusts will not – for now – be able to make profits directly from school budgets, but they will be able to appoint their cronies at monstrous salaries, without any public control, and provide profits indirectly to the "sponsor" and their friends by deciding where the school will buy equipment or services – computers, building repairs, staffing agencies and so on.

Despite the government's "parent power" rhetoric, the introduction of trust schools will place parents at the mercy of second hand car salesmen and religious cranks. Trust schools' power to decide their own admissions policy – even within the framework of an admissions code – could mean children having to travel long distances because they have been rejected by local schools. The chaos that parents and children already face, particularly in London, will spread.

In a system that parallels privatisation in the NHS, local education authorities will in future become "commissioners, not providers" of schools. The white paper outlined steps to accelerate this process of floating off schools, including making inspections tougher and labelling many more schools as "failing" or – another elastic concept – "coasting" to accelerate their closure and transfer to private ownership. No wonder the policy was applauded by the Conservatives and greeted with dismay by many Labour backbenchers.

Inspections would also be more frequent, with a hotline to Ofsted set up to encourage parents to complain about schools. In case anybody doubts the purpose, the government threatens to "bear down on those schools that do not recognise their weaknesses".

The white paper set a time scale of just a year for schools put into "special measures" to improve. It recommended that local education authorities employ methods such as removing the head, deputies, governing body or school budget, putting the school under the control of one of its neighbours (and competitors). Education authorities must consider, "in certain cases, immediate closure of the school", the white paper said.

These dramatic interventions will not improve schools – they are more likely to send them nose-diving into chaos. School inspectors, the school improvement partners and local education authorities are to become the policemen and agents of privatisation.

Under cover of parent "choice" and "diversity"

As if these measures to push schools into trust status were not enough, a simple majority of governors – perhaps as few as half a dozen people – will be able to decide to become a trust school. It will be all too easy for a cabal to plot to take over a school governing body – get this parent or that member of staff elected, co-opt a local businessman or religious fanatic – and before anybody realises what is happening, they vote to hand power to a trust.

The government's proposals will also let any group of parents set up a new trust school. The education authority will have a duty to help such groups of parents, including providing buildings or letting the new trust school move into a wing of an existing school. The government is even setting up a dedicated capital fund to provide new buildings for new trust schools, however wasteful this might be. A Schools Commissioner will deal with local authorities that fail to cooperate – the authority must help the parents' group even if there are already enough school places in the area.

Education authorities will have to seek out schools to close in order to ensure there are not too many surplus places in the area. This means that a gang of influential parents could draw on public money to open a trust school – and bring about the closure of the neighbourhood school that other parents and pupils rely on. In typical Blair-speak, the white paper says, "Local authorities will...consider whether the capital assets released could be used to inject new dynamism into the system."

Allowing parents to set up schools in this way might appear not too different to the diversity of schools provision in countries such as Denmark and the Netherlands, but this will not be the case here. The white paper's authors are clear that any old group of parents will not do – although a few Muslim schools might be included to make the policy appear even handed, the government does not want environmentalists, socialists or creative arts cooperatives setting up schools. At the time of writing, ministers were still looking for a legal formula to define "inappropriate" trusts.

This bias has a Thatcherite pedigree. In the 1980s a group of progressive parents tried to use the Conservative legislation that created City Technology Colleges – the precursors of the city academies – to establish a publicly funded school that followed the distinctive Steiner educational philosophy. This was quickly disallowed.

The white paper is thin on logic and even thinner on evidence, but it is a classic text for students of New Labour ideology. It creates a tissue of apparent logic by tying together things that don't actually connect, as if the links were self-evident. Privatisation is dressed up as "empowerment" or "choice and diversity" – although testing, the National Curriculum and Ofsted retain as tight a grip as ever:

> We need to create a schools system shaped by parents that delivers excellence and equity – developing the talents and potential of every child, regardless of their background – a system that can rapidly open to good new providers who can help make this happen.

Higher Standards, Better Schools for All
The white paper is full of rhetorical appeal. It is scattered with phrases designed to appeal to a broad constituency – more personalised learning, parent and community involvement, stretching the brightest pupils, better schools for the most disadvantaged areas – but this is a cosmetic exercise designed to attract the gullible and minimise dissent in the Labour Party's ranks. Blair's education ministers must realise that privatised schools, each with its own admissions policy, will create even more of a dog-eat-dog situation, causing the greatest damage to schools in the most troubled and deprived neighbourhoods.

The switch to trust schools provides an answer to the Confederation of British Industry's demand that a much greater part of the national schools' budget should come the way of private companies.[13] But the main purpose of Blair's reforms is probably to ensure that schooling more directly serves employers' needs through a more vocational curriculum.

Comprehensive schools: a new vision
Blair and his friends have gone to great lengths to undermine comprehensive schools – the prime minister's former official spokesperson, Alastair Campbell, dubbed them "bog-standard comprehensives". We have to insist on the principle of schools – and colleges and universities – that are open to all, where access is not through money, influence or social status. We also have to develop a vision of what comprehensive schools can become.

As international comparisons show, comprehensive schools have been a success. Where children are divided into different levels of school, this inevitably discriminates against manual workers and minorities.

Even in Britain the benefits of comprehensive schools are well established where they have not been undermined by subtle divisions and market competition.

In Scotland private schools – attended by a smaller percentage of children than in England – do achieve higher exam results than state schools, which are all comprehensive. This reflects parents' occupations and education. At the private schools 72 percent of parents are in the wealthiest social class I and just 2 percent had left school at age 15. At the state schools, however, only 26 percent of parents were in social class I and 24 percent had left school at 15. But once these differences of occupation and educational level are taken into account, the adjusted results are almost identical. The data for children whose father is in a non-manual occupation, and with both parents educated to age 17 or older, shows very little difference between the results at the private schools and the state comprehensives. At the independent schools 61 percent of pupils pass five or more Highers (the university entrance qualification), compared with 57 percent in the comprehensive schools. And this comparison does not even take into account the fact that the independent schools have already selected pupils by "ability".[14]

An education system can respond to a wide range of interests and abilities without segregating children into different schools. The early comprehensives – and many to this day – included a wide range of facilities that all students could use, such as car mechanics workshops and childcare areas. They did not have a two-track curriculum, but students doing car mechanics and childcare could also study drama, history or Spanish.

The notion of "specialist schools" began in imitation of "magnet schools" in the US – higher-status city schools that could reject all but the most talented and motivated students from the poorest areas. Even though specialist schools have (generally) taken a different turn in England, they are clearly not working as a means of fostering particular talents. Government inspectors have discovered that, however good a school is overall, there is generally nothing very "special" about the school's specialism. With few exceptions, it is absurd to select 10 year olds for a particular school because of a "potential" for technology or sport or languages. Do they not also have other talents and potential? Might not other children have hidden potential? There are two obvious alternatives:

- Develop high-level facilities in specific schools and colleges, as specialist centres which are open to all children from surrounding schools on a particular day in the week, during evenings and at the weekend. Allow all interested young people in a town to spend a day a week in the specialist music or drama or languages centre.
- Establish weekend and holiday courses, including residential courses, to extend the gifts and talents of all children, not just summer schools for the few who are labelled gifted or talented as at present. As well as fully promoting talents which are already apparent, often because of parents and private tuition, we should set out to develop the undiscovered talents of all young people.

Without the constant pressure of tests and targets, schools would have more chance of creating new opportunities through partnerships with sports clubs, drama and music groups. Some interesting educational partnerships could be developed with places of work, offering more than just premature job training. Local councils and community groups could involve schools in investigating real problems and proposing solutions. Schools could be involved in community-based research and design, and help to enhance local health and leisure facilities. There are many rich possibilities.

CHAPTER 5

Standardised schools,excluded students

It is easy to join in the chorus when politicians and journalists are baying for blood. A moral panic about young people's behaviour has built up in recent years, and anxiety about disorderly schools is loaded with nostalgia for the "good old days". But banning "hoodies" from shopping malls is not just farcical – it stigmatises young people as criminal and dangerous.

School discipline was probably easier to impose in days gone by – though each generation seems to put a different date on when that was. A recently retired colleague from the north of Scotland tells how his friend at school was beaten every morning for getting his spellings wrong. The teacher said he was wicked and in need of redemption, though the beatings never did cure his sinfulness.

Teachers rarely take such a damning approach nowadays, and such a punishment is illegal, but there are modern parallels to my Scottish colleague's tale. The situation is exacerbated when uniform standards of behaviour are expected within a high-stakes exam-bound system that puts implacable pressures on teachers. It is difficult, in such an environment, to step back and critically reflect on what is happening.

For teachers facing daily conflict and stress, the "common sense" response is to blame young people – and not to ask questions about the situation as a whole. It is easy to take for granted traditional features of schools – passive learning, rigid timetables, repetitive exercises, archaic disciplinary codes – as if they were natural or inevitable, and to regard those learners who find it hardest to adjust as deviants. Pupils can be regarded as bad, mad or simply ill, but all these conclusions result from seeing the individual behaviour in isolation from the cultural situation and the immediate school context.

It is dangerous to look at situations one-sidedly. We should avoid making judgements about individual pupils' behaviours without considering the school and social context and the sum total of a young person's life experiences. One-sided diagnoses usually result in simplistic answers that don't get to the heart of the problem. Rather than castigating the behaviour of pupils, we need to look at the social change that is making young people very different to previous generations, and to question whether schools have adapted successfully to new conditions.

Substantial educational change has occurred in many parts of the world. England is overflowing with the rhetoric of school improvement but much of this is intensification, not thoughtful change. They are speeding up the conveyor belt, when they should be rethinking education for the children of the 21st century.

There is a useful distinction between a *medical* (or psychological) model and a *social* (or environmental) one, as alternative ways of looking at school problems.[1] The medical model focuses entirely on the individual as a problem. The social model looks at the young person's life and the school environment as well. It does not automatically assume that the individual is in the wrong, or that the school situation cannot be changed. This distinction provides a way of looking critically and openly at difficult situations.

School exclusions: the example of African-Caribbean students

A classic example is the high frequency of exclusions for African-Caribbean students, especially boys.[2] This goes well beyond teachers' normal reactions to adolescents. When teachers are under pressure, they are more likely to react instinctively to behaviour they may not identify with or make sense of. Cultural difference leads to misunderstanding, which is often compounded by deeply ingrained and unconscious racial fears and stereotyping.

It is easy for teachers to interpret mock aggression, directness in expression and general bravado as dangerous or disruptive. Ill-considered reactions such as public shaming arouse an inevitable reaction, and soon the situation is out of hand.

Even minor incidents are blown up and the conflict results in the student's expulsion from school. In many cases, nobody stops to investigate why, or to ask whether there is something wrong with the school environment. It is simply put down to the pupil's malevolence or a desire to disrupt. But the repeated failure of a school to question this recurrent pattern amounts to racism.

The pressures on teachers to secure maximum performance are now so severe that there is less time to reflect and a greater likelihood of writing off young people as impossible to educate. Nevertheless the teaching profession has to resist the pressure it has been put under, and to examine what positive steps can be taken towards cultural inclusion. A broad strategy would include:

- ensuring that the curriculum reflects cultural diversity, whether that is maths or science or history
- developing anti-racist understanding – and the courage to challenge racism when it occurs – among students, staff and school management
- making steps to respond to cases of underachievement and disengagement with genuine empathy and dialogue, as well as academic guidance and learning resources
- providing more opportunities for active learning, so that challenging ideas are grounded in experience

- creating recreational and cultural opportunities in schools which demonstrate a living respect for Black pupils and their families

Punish and expel

The situation for African-Caribbean students, though probably the most extreme, is only part of a wider pattern. All kinds of young people are misjudged on the basis of body language or other behaviour linked to ethnicity, class, gender or youth culture. Government ministers are acutely aware of the long-term consequences of absenteeism or exclusion, but they seem incapable of realising that there might be something wrong with the schooling they have imposed. They try to cure the problem with a stiff dose of punishment.

The absurdity of the government's position could be seen when former education minister Ruth Kelly announced a "zero tolerance" policy – she has borrowed from a US policy that leads to hundreds of thousands of young Americans (mainly Black and Hispanic) being jailed for petty offences. Equally absurd was the policy proposing strong measures to force disaffected youngsters back into school – followed by equally strong measures to isolate them in special behaviour units when they got there. As is evident from the US, the rhetoric and the consequences both tend to escalate.

The 2006 Education and Inspections Bill goes to great lengths to strengthen school discipline. Its proposals include detentions on Saturdays and Sundays, the requirement to obey any instruction that is not illegal from any adult working in the school, the right for schools to take parents to court and demand that parenting orders be imposed on them, and the right of teachers to use force even to prevent pupils damaging their own property.

Another government response is to punish the parents. This doesn't help those who are struggling to cope, and fails to challenge either the school situation or the existence of chronic poverty.

We are now faced with a criminalisation of young people in two parallel senses: the tendency, exacerbated by the media, to regard a wide range of juvenile behaviour as inherently criminal and the introduction of punitive sanctions to regulate this behaviour.

The pressures become particularly difficult for teachers, who have to deal with irreconcilable tensions, but it is not helped by a perverse kind of union militancy by some (but by no means all) members of one of the teacher trade unions that cannot think beyond blaming and punishing young people.

It is misleading to simply put school exclusions down to a changing youth culture, though it is clear that traditional schooling is out of step with young people's expectations and lifestyles. Nor do the exclusions reflect a sudden increase in disruptive behaviour. Contrary to myth, only 1 percent of exclusions are triggered by physical confrontations with teachers. There are also large differences between schools.

The introduction of market competition between schools in England and Wales led to a 450 percent increase in permanent exclusions between 1990 and 1995, as schools came under pressure to secure high positions in league tables and avoid bad publicity. Exclusion is the price many young people and families have paid for schools being put into the marketplace.

None of this is intended to suggest that serious problems do not exist, but more imaginative solutions have to be found, including more interesting ways of learning and a change in the way schools are organised to create a better sense of community, agency and belonging (see Chapter 6). The teaching unions' longstanding demand for smaller classes is equally important here, and particularly where issues of poverty and racism compound the difficulties faced.

A cycle of rejection

A recent study of excluded and disaffected students in Lancashire schools paid special attention to the young people's own stories and those of their parents.[3] They described what it felt like to be excluded from class – being "put on ice". Contrary to the assumption that they couldn't care less, they felt like outcasts, unable to move forward: "You sit there and do nothing... It didn't do nothing to change me." Erratic attendance led to sarcastic comments from a few teachers: "Oh you've finally decided to join us today then, have you?" Students found reintegration a lonely business and recovery difficult. One form teacher welcomed back a long-term truant by encouraging a slow handclap.

The young people told of good teachers who explained things well, were "fair to everyone" and had a "sense of humour", and of others who were shrill and used humiliation to maintain order. When the researchers asked them to draw their situations, it became clear that many found school a sad and depressing experience. Many of the images were bleak, picturing stressed and isolated children and shouting teachers. Smelly lavatories featured in many drawings, along with images of schools as prisons.

We can neither write off these experiences and representations nor simply take them at face value, but we must examine them in relationship to an educational regime that is socially damaging.

There are also some very positive initiatives from schools that have tried to break down the barriers, such as the Rochdale school I visited, where the head and deputies had moved out of their offices and into an empty classroom, removing the door to give students, teachers and parents open access. Another school built a conservatory, so that parents could visit the headteacher without feeling intimidated facing him across his desk. Both initiatives radically transformed the school culture by rebuilding relationships – and helped to bring about dramatic improvements in learning and achievement.

The myth of Attention Deficit Hyperactivity Disorder (ADHD)

In a scientific age it is more acceptable to say that someone is suffering from a disease than to label them bad or mad. This is exactly what has happened to young people who just cannot settle in class.[4]

The "disease" of ADHD was unknown 30 years ago. It first emerged in 1976 as a medical syndrome under the name of hyperkinesis. Its epicentre is the US, but it is chilling to learn of a 76-fold increase in prescriptions for methylphenidate (eg Ritalin) in England over the past ten years. Globally, ADHD is a massive growth industry, with prescriptions worth nearly $3 billion.

In fact, the "symptoms" of ADHD consist essentially of behaviours that teachers find a nuisance in class. Doctors are invited to make a diagnosis of an *inattention type* of ADHD or a *hyperactivity/impulsivity type*, or a combination. For the first, according to a US Department of Health manual, children can show any six of the following behaviours:

- often does not give close attention to details or makes careless mistakes in schoolwork, work or other activities
- often has trouble keeping attention on tasks or play activities
- often does not seem to listen when spoken to directly
- often does not follow instructions, and fails to finish schoolwork, chores or duties
- often has trouble organising activities
- often avoids, dislikes or doesn't want to do things that take a lot of mental effort for a long period of time – such as schoolwork or homework
- often loses things needed for tasks and activities – such as toys, school assignments, pencils, books or tools
- is often easily distracted
- is often forgetful in daily activities[5]

The symptoms for the hyperactivity/impulsivity type include fidgeting, getting up from your seat, having trouble playing quietly, blurting out answers before the question is finished and interrupting other people's conversations.

Aren't these "symptoms" perfectly natural in many children and adolescents? It is not unusual for children to be hyperactive, distractible and impulsive. These characteristics gradually decline with age – though I see many of the "symptoms" in myself on a bad day after too much coffee. There is a spectrum of behaviours and emotional states that are perfectly natural but become especially problematic in strained environments such as schools. The US Department of Health manual concedes:

Signs of the disorder may be minimal or absent when the person is under strict control, is in a novel setting, is engaged in especially interesting activities, is in a one-to-one situation (eg in the clinician's office), or while the person experiences frequent rewards for appropriate behaviours.

It is always important, with any kind of learning difficulty or special need, to examine the context and not simply concentrate on the individual as some kind of specimen. We need to use an environmental/social model to gain full understanding, rather than an individualistic psychological/medical model. This is certainly the case with behavioural difficulties and is even true with a physical impairment – the impact of being in a wheelchair is exacerbated by inaccessible buildings and negative social responses. It is blinkered and irresponsible to simply blame the student for disaffection or lack of concentration when the curriculum itself is boring.

This is not to suggest that some children's behaviour doesn't present enormous problems to teachers, but these problems are the result of contradictions between the individual – a result of biological, domestic and cultural factors – and the school environment. Slapping on the ADHD label avoids examining the particularity of these influences and contradictions.

A change of diet has been shown to bring an improvement in behaviour. Changes in the learning environment including more active learning, more decision making by learners and increased use of outdoor environments can alter behaviours and reduce the possibility of conflict. The natural response of many adolescents to learning with too little collective activity or engaged problem solving is to interact and engage in other ways – it is too easy to read this as a symptom of "ADHD".

ADHD is a peculiar "disease" in that it leaves no physical or chemical traces, during life or – autopsies have shown – after death. The brain scan research that has claimed to detect abnormalities has been conducted on individuals dosed on various drugs, and is as likely to result from the drugs themselves.[6] Many reasons for the spread of "ADHD" relate to life under fast capitalism.

- The pharmaceutical industry has a massive stake. It sponsors organisations which interpret troublesome behaviours as a neurological disorder, for which the answer is lucrative drug prescriptions.
- Poor nutrition, including too many additives and a lack of omega-3 oils, can be very damaging. On the other hand, improved diet has brought about more settled behaviour. The food industry has brought about harmful changes in diet in the past 30 years in pursuit of increased profit.
- Greater domestic instability may be partly responsible.
- Developments in TV production and video games may affect the neurological development of children. Pressure from advertisers has gradually led to many more "jolts per minute" to grab maximum attention, giving rise to a short attention span culture.
- Play is disappearing from many children's lives, and especially play involving movement over distances, physical activity, imagination and impromptu planning. Since the drugs prescribed for ADHD suppress the drive to play, diagnosed children have a double-dose of harm.
- The accountability and target culture in schools has put enormous pressure on children, teachers and parents. In the US the accountability drive from the 1970s directly coincided with the rise of the "ADHD" diagnosis. Parents and teachers become anxious if children are not performing "at or above grade level".
- Children are being expected to show a capacity for concentrated learning which is unreasonable for their age, and those who don't are regarded as defective.

Many classroom conflicts would be resolvable if teachers were allowed to think creatively about the curriculum and learning, and how to work with young people. Some young people need specific help and support in dealing with domestic, relationship or health problems, not simply a daily dose of Ritalin. In a very few cases, medication might be necessary to alleviate behavioural difficulties but it is unlikely to be sustained if their other problems are not dealt with.

US author and former teacher Thomas Armstrong, whose work is the main source of the list of reasons behind ADHD cited above, suggests we should regard children labelled with ADHD as "canaries in the coal mine". Just as canaries once helped miners to detect gas, these children should provide "biocultural feedback" about life under fast capitalism and high-pressure schooling:

> Were the field of attention deficit hyperactivity disorder to have a "poster boy" to promote its cause, it would surely have to be Calvin from the US Calvin and Hobbes cartoon strips. In one of my favourites, Calvin is sitting at a school desk, utterly bored. Eventually, he shouts out to the teacher and all of his classmates: "BO-RING." In the last panel, we see Calvin being sent to the principal, saying: "Yeh yeh… kill the messenger."[7]

Part 2:

Where do we go from here?

CHAPTER 6

Community and democracy

The quality of life at school is not a marginal issue. After all, young people are compelled to spend a large part of their life in school, so it should be a happy and exciting place. It is their first experience of living and working together in a large social group. Schools should provide young people with a sense of community and an experience of democratic participation. How well do they currently fulfil these roles?

The ethos in schools has improved in some ways since the 1950s, but they have not kept pace with changes in society at large. Physical punishment has been abolished, but classrooms are still very tightly regulated. Behaviour is often discussed as a discrete problem, as if it were unaffected by the quality of school life and the curriculum. High pressure "delivery" of a standardised curriculum, constant messages of failure and little attempt to connect to life often produce alienation and frustration.

It would be misleading to claim that government policy is not concerned with school ethos – indeed there are many references to it in official documents. The trouble is, the advice is based on tacit assumptions – authoritarian norms and expectations, large classes and impersonal schools. It is right to worry if schools are chaotic, but insisting on them being *orderly* is misleading, since there are many different kinds of *order*. An *orderly* school could be harmonious and stimulating – or repressive and depressing.

When studying successful inner-city schools, I found the key word was not so much "order" as "respect". This emerged in many ways in the school culture:

- the display of children's photographs and their work
- the quality of personal relationships
- reaching out to parents
- active celebration of heritage and youth cultures
- the display and use of community languages
- signs of engagement with local communities
- involvement of students in writing the behaviour code

- a refusal to write off difficult and troubled youngsters
- establishing social and recreational spaces[1]

Respect inevitably has a cultural and political dimension. Young people soon see through tokenistic displays of a few cultural artefacts – the "steel drums, samosas and saris" level of multiculturalism – when a school is not genuinely open to living cultures. Genuine respect requires courage on the part of teachers and heads, requiring them to investigate and challenge possible signs of racism rather than sweeping them under the carpet or blaming the victim for being young and feeling angry.

Official advice on improving school ethos is often functionalist, as if it were only a means to an end – the road to higher test results. A genuine concern would require us to consider how we might really enrich young lives. Similarly, official guidance on parental involvement tends to be based on the assumption of a one-way relationship, as if the parents were merely a vehicle to get children to school, homework in hand. A serious partnership between schools and families depends on reaching out and connecting to the reality of parents' lives, and discussing how school facilities could contribute to the struggle to survive and fight poverty.

It is extremely blinkered to think schools can somehow stay the same however much society changes. Kids are not the same as they were. This does not mean that schools should try to match the rapid fire of the video game or the spectacular violence of many films, but we do need to make school learning more active and engaged.

Teachers, parents and students need to discuss openly how schools could work as social and learning communities rather than as knowledge factories or bureaucratic organisations. This is not to deny the importance of achievement, but given the moral panic about social and family breakdown, it is time to examine what schools might do to create a sense of stability and belonging.

With these thoughts in mind, a major conference in Germany in 1995 agreed this mission statement:

School is a House of Learning:

- a place where everybody is welcome, where learners and teachers are accepted in their individuality
- a place where people are allowed time to grow up, to take care of one another and be treated with respect
- a place whose rooms invite you to stay, offer you the chance to learn, and stimulate you to learn and show initiative
- a place where diversions and mistakes are allowed, but where evaluation in the form of feedback gives you a sense of direction
- a place for intensive work, and where it feels good to learn
- a place where learning is infectious[2]

In Britain too there are many good examples of schools that live up to these ideals. There is no contradiction between community values and successful learning. In fact, a welcoming school environment is even more important if the neighbourhood is fragile and troubled. Successful inner city schools have many symbols of belonging – children's photographs, birthdays, cultural symbols, school trips and outdoor activity holidays.

An active sense of ownership is a key feature. In a comprehensive in Stockton-on-Tees, in the north east of England, a group of students took action to improve their environment. They called themselves "Enviromob" and planned their initiatives inside and around the school autonomously, but with teachers' support. Enviromob got half the school to volunteer in their biggest initiative, planning and carrying out improvements including murals and gardens. Democratic pupil involvement, with help from parent volunteers, has also thoroughly transformed a primary school in Glasgow, where even the toilets were magnificent after pupils put up curtains, mirrors and flowers.[3]

Student voice

Schools are not usually good places to learn democracy. The introduction of "education for citizenship" has provided arguments for some basic democratic practices in the running of schools. Unfortunately, student representative councils, which are supposed to teach democracy, often do the reverse, making young people cynical and disillusioned when their proposals are frustrated. They are often marginal in their impact on school life and the curriculum. "Circle time" in primary schools is another example of a democratic reform, creating a space for more open debate, but all too often it is subverted into a further means of upholding discipline.

The *student voice* project, aimed at involving young people in evaluating their education, has the potential to transform power relationships. But inserted into an authoritarian system dominated by inspection and top-down control, it could easily have a different result. Major power differences can also be found within the student body – inequalities of class, ethnicity and gender or sexuality can privilege some and marginalise others. We need to ask some basic critical questions about democratic reforms in school, and about the "student voice" – who is allowed to speak? To whom? What about? What action follows? What happens if aspirations are not realised? What role does the student voice play in the structure of power?[4]

Classic writings on community are often based on nostalgic and mystical notions of an organic village community – a classless rural idyll that never existed. Democratising schools in a complex 21st century society requires a representative forum, but also alternative spaces in which minority experiences can be exchanged and particular voices clearly heard.

The problem with secondary schools

The sense of alienation is generally higher when pupils move from primary to secondary school. Many thoughtful steps have been taken to aid the transition, such as pre-transfer visits for pupils, and teachers put a lot of effort into pastoral care and guidance, but this is a sticking-plaster solution if the issue of school structure is overlooked.

The structure of secondary schools is based on that of traditional grammar schools – specialist subject departments – but with various pastoral and support systems added on. This structure worked reasonably well in the grammar schools, which were normally smaller and only taught a small section of the population. But it is under enormous strain in large urban schools serving a more diverse student body. To many young people, school life is like drifting around a major airport.

It is worth asking how most adults would cope with 12 or 15 different bosses a week, and being herded from room to room once every hour. Why is this so low on the school reform agenda? Instead of denouncing young people as yobs and their families as dysfunctional, it would be more helpful to reshape schools as nurturing communities.

Lessons can be learned from other countries. In Scandinavia schools for teenagers avoid the fragmented relationships of British secondary schools. Most teachers are qualified in several subjects, and teach fewer classes but each for a longer time.

In Norway teachers are grouped into school years, not subject departments.[5] Typically, 100 students aged 14 to 15 are taught and looked after by five or six teachers – between them, they cover the whole curriculum and provide pastoral care and guidance. The team includes expertise in learning support, and is largely self-managing. They can easily rearrange the timetable for visits and special projects. Each class has a main teacher, for a third of the week, and only four or five teachers altogether. Teachers are not faced with hundreds of different pupils every week. Teachers and pupils know each other very well, and relationships and trust make behaviour problems rare and negotiable. The situation is much less stressful for teachers and learners. It is a social community and a learning community.

In the US a grassroots reform movement has led to the replacement of giant city schools by thousands of secondary schools on a human scale.[6] In some cases, several small schools are located in different parts of a single building – formerly a large high school – sharing some common facilities. There is solid evidence to show that smaller schools are better for all young people in terms of personal and social development. For working class and minority students in particular, achievement is higher and the staying-on rate improves.

Despite the tight specialisation, a few British secondary schools have also found successful ways to reduce the problem. Their solutions include:

- A number of classes or year groups are formed into a "mini-school" or "school within a school" with a dedicated group of teachers for most academic and pastoral purposes.
- Younger classes are taught and looked after by a single teacher for several subjects, making up around 40 percent of the timetable. The students have a limited number of other teachers, and can return to their home base at breaks and lunchtimes.[7]

It is also important to look at what happens at breaks and lunch times: are there recreational areas, or are students simply pushed outside?

Breaking down the barriers to learning

Sociologists such as Pierre Bourdieu have argued that young people growing up in areas of poverty lack the "cultural capital" needed for success at school.[8] This does not mean they have less culture, but that their interests and knowledge don't count for much within the school. It is not surprising that teachers can generalise from dramatic incidents and conclude that the neighbourhood they serve is nothing but a concrete jungle full of dysfunctional families and drug-crazed youths.

Teachers rarely have the chance to explore the community for its positive features, such as interests and social networks. A pioneering project undertaken by Luis Moll and his colleagues with a Puerto Rican community in the US revealed rich funds of knowledge of which teachers had been unaware, and on which they then began to build.[9] In Britain this lack of understanding of the community may be even more of a problem in run down working class housing estates than in the multiethnic inner city – even though schools' knowledge of Asian or Caribbean cultures may be static or superficial.

Exploring the cultural and social assets of the community can also reveal different patterns of learning. In the community, learning often resembles an apprenticeship model, where specific skills are acquired in real situations out of a genuine desire and need. School learning normally reverses this, disconnecting sub-skills from any larger purpose, or simply inventing a "context" as a kind of background decoration.

There is enormous untapped potential for working closely with parents. There is a tendency to see this one-sidedly, for example sending reading books home with young children so that parents can given them extra practice. But the teacher-parent partnership is equally important in reconnecting school learning with the everyday literacy children encounter when they go shopping. Teachers need the flexibility to do this without constantly worrying about the next target.

Community schools

Tony Blair has trivialised the term "community school" by applying it to non-religious schools in general. But there is a long tradition of genuine community schools that have struggled to overcome the barriers between compulsory 9 to 4 schooling and wider learning in the neighbourhood. At the most basic level this has simply involved shared accommodation, essentially as an economy measure, with evening classes in the school building or sports teams using the gym. But there are many richer possibilities that are crucially important in areas of poverty where there is greater social or cultural distance between parents and teachers. Examples include:

● Primary schools with playgroups and toy libraries, so that social contacts between parents and teachers are built even before the child starts school.

- A Rochdale primary school whose community centre provides a social and learning space for Muslim women and where some mothers become classroom helpers and then train as classroom assistants.
- A centre for elderly people, housed in a Gateshead secondary school. In one project, school students and pensioners went to visit the Beamish open-air museum together, checking image against memory and writing oral history to share with similar projects in Europe.

The concept of extended schools is basically a positive one, but in discussing how to open up the school as a public space, we have to think sharply about the geography of power. Spaces are appropriated, accessed and controlled in different ways, according to degrees of influence and prestige.

Scotland's integrated community schools for working class neighbourhoods bring together teachers, health workers and social services. They provide possibilities for all kinds of change – but there is a danger of doing things to people rather than building up their initiative and confidence. At worst, when diverse professionals gather together to "sort out Mrs Mackenzie", this can prove overpowering and alienating.

We should also pay heed to a recent primary school survey in Brent, north west London, on the question of after-school care. The pupils said they would prefer better pay for their mums so they could work shorter hours and get home earlier.

An empowerment model of community school means helping local people to take initiatives, and democratically run community education and events. One German model of citizenship education involves problem solving, not as an exercise but based on a real problem. The town council or health centre brings its problem to the school; the students then present possible solutions to the officials and community. A Northumberland school persuaded the local council to set aside regeneration funds to respond to students' ideas on how to improve their town.

Communities and learning

Community learning can enable people to assert their collective power in order to challenge inertia and injustice. Community video is underused in Britain. The Brazilian organisation CECIP (the Centre for the Creation of Popular Image) was established in response to Brazilian educationalist Paulo Freire's idea that "reading the word is reading the world".[10] Freire's thinking was extended from the printed and written word to modern media, providing extremely poor people with video equipment and skills. Participants choose the theme of their projects, then film, edit and finally show their video to large audiences in the open air, leading to lively discussion and collective action. One community challenged the city council's failure to clear rubbish and free the area of pollution. Women's groups exposed the poor quality of maternity care and healthcare in public hospitals. Homeless teenagers wrote sex and health education resources for younger children living on the streets.

Radical community education can challenge basic notions of where knowledge comes from, showing that the funds of knowledge within a neighbourhood are as important as school-based knowledge. This affects mainstream school learning too. After visiting a war memorial some Australian students examined grandparents' letters, newspaper cuttings and documents to see what the wars had really been like. This showed up the differences between the national myths glorifying war and the brutal reality. [11]

Volunteering and community placements can also involve substantial learning, although we need to sharpen critical perspectives by raising issues of power and social justice. Otherwise we are simply applying sticking plaster to social problems through charitable work.

All this goes well beyond the version of community learning encouraged by officially sanctioned education for citizenship. Education for democratic citizenship involves fostering a critical understanding – and direct experience of organising to make the world a better place.

The apple pie is baking in the oven and the smell of bubbling cinnamon, sugar and apples fills the air and makes the kitchen feel warm and cosy on this cold and windy November morning. Groups of students sit with their teachers round large farm tables with tablecloths, centrepieces and plates painted with delicate blue flowers.

This is a very different start to the school day than a literacy or numeracy hour. The one-acre urban garden and its kitchen provide a curriculum that connects students with the earth, the environment, and adults from the neighbourhood. The children are literally coming to their senses.

The teachers call it a "seed to table" experience – preparing the soil, planting, tending and harvesting organic crops and then cooking them. In this year-round process, for an hour and a half each week, children develop an understanding of environmental stewardship, the interconnectedness of people to one another, to their community and to the earth, and an appreciation of the value and joy of meaningful work.

We want to slow them down, to bust a hole in their day. Our students are so stimulated with stuff all day long that they don't always stop and get the feeling of doing ordinary things for pleasure.

I wanted the students to have time to play, to be outdoors. I wanted a place to keep them young for a little while longer.

Within this practical environment, the children learn science, from soil erosion to photosynthesis. They have made proposals to prevent erosion on a local hillside. They write journals based on their work. It is developing confidence and self-esteem. It is a great equaliser, allowing children who have been less successful academically to gain in prestige.

Community volunteers play a critical role, ensuring that children can work in small groups and providing caring adults for them to learn from and interact with.

The Edible Schoolyard was the idea of a local chef who wanted to give children the chance to grow food and take part in preparing their own lunches. She was concerned that children had no idea where food came from, and needed the experience of making food and eating together, which was missing in many homes. The project has been a model for other schools.

We need a curriculum that offers alternatives to the fast-food messages that saturate our contemporary culture. These messages tell us that food is cheap and abundant, that abundance is permanent, that resources are infinite, that it's OK to waste, that standardisation is more important than quality and that speed is a virtue above all others.

What we need is a systematic overhaul of education inspired by the Slow Food movement. "Slow schools" would promote community by allowing room for discovery and for paying attention – concentration and judgement and all the other slow food values that testing cannot measure.[12]

Martin Luther King School, Berkeley California

CHAPTER 7

'Literacy' is just not good enough

It is about seven years since government officials turned England's primary schools upside down by insisting that there was only one way to teach reading – the stereotyped literacy hour. Teachers were given a blast of quick-fix training and expected to obediently deliver the set pattern. Their existing expertise was ignored – though fortunately many were bold enough to adapt the literacy hour according to their professional judgement.

Until recently schools rarely used the term *literacy*, preferring *English* or *language* or *reading and writing*. The recent change of terminology has encouraged more artificial ways of teaching reading based on sub-skills – putting the parts before the whole.

Too much learning in schools consists of exercises to acquire skills, although in other settings we learn skills incidentally or because the situation demands them. The predominance of artificial exercises is a central characteristic of government literacy strategies. Exercises are sometimes useful as a form of intensive practice, but literacy as a meaningful activity should be at the centre.[1]

The most successful young readers have generally had a rich experience of real reading at home. Parents and siblings have told them stories and read them books. They went to libraries to choose picture books even before they could walk. Their carers drew attention to print in the environment – shop signs, labels on the tomato ketchup. (These are supposedly "middle class" habits but are much more widespread.)

Reading and writing are built on spoken language. This may seem obvious but it is especially important for bilingual pupils and other children speaking varieties of English that differ from Standard English. The literacy hour has made it much more difficult for teachers to connect literacy to spoken language, with respect for other languages and dialects. Language development depends on rich experience, but this doesn't fit well with the rigid structure of the literacy hour. Bilingual children in particular need activities that are rich in experiences, spoken language and literacy – best provided through a more integrated curriculum connecting with family and community experience.

The literacy hour was supposed to overcome a learning disadvantage of manual workers' children, especially boys. In fact, by presenting literacy as an artificial acquisition of discrete sub-skills, it has missed the point. It is not surprising that government targets have not been met. Although official guidance now acknowledges the idea of pleasure in reading once more, this is difficult to achieve against a backdrop of detailed prescription.

Reading to order

The literacy strategy rigidly defines the content to be taught each term. This is even worse than the original National Curriculum, which had an overall expectation for each key stage. Now prescription means that all schools work to the same blueprint. This has been reinforced by cascade-type training, monitoring and a continuous stream of training videos, manuals, workbooks and websites to control teachers' decisions.

Even when teachers are encouraged to use exploratory discussion, this is undermined by the number of objectives they have to cover. The emphasis on transmitting discrete skills and items of knowledge leads to didactic teaching, where children's responses are tightly constrained. Recent research showed that nine out of ten of pupils' spoken contributions were less than three words long.[2] This affects the way teachers view literacy, and the way they view themselves. It is turning them into mere conduits for a centrally imposed curriculum, rather than reflective professionals.

Language is seen as the sum of its parts. Pupils are encouraged to regard texts as a collection of different bits, and writing as a box of tricks. Young writers are required to "add detail" and use "powerful verbs" as tricks for good writing. The artificiality and fragmentary nature of this approach has been sharply criticised by children's author Philip Pullman:

> They think that reading consists of using a range of strategies to decode, selecting, retrieving, deducing, inferring, interpreting… That's it. That's all. Nothing else. That's what they want children of 11 to do when they read… Enjoyment just doesn't feature in the list of things you have to do…
>
> Another unit of work is built around two short stories and part of a novel. It's not expected that the children will have their own copies of the complete texts… Books exist in order to be taken apart and laid out in pieces like Lego. The children have to list "the features of a good story opening" and "check this against the criteria for a good opening – does it fulfil all of these?"
>
> I can't say it clearly enough: this is not how it works. Writing doesn't happen like this. You cannot write a good story by building up a list of effective openings.
>
> Stories are written to beguile, to entertain, to amuse, to move, to enchant, to horrify, to delight, to anger, to make us wonder. They are not written so that we can make a 50-word summary of the whole plot, or find five synonyms for the descriptive words. That sort of thing would make you hate reading, and turn away from such a futile activity with disgust. In the words of Ruskin, it's slaves' work, unredeemed.[3]

Analysing texts is sometimes useful, but it now dominates reading and writing, and the way children are taught to see it. By contrast, Pullman says real writing is "like fishing in a boat at night".

Even though tests for 11 year olds were simplified to make the literacy hour appear a success, test results soon got stuck and failed to meet targets, so now we are on the edge of another quick-fix reform. Professional teaching skills will once again be overlooked if primary teachers are ordered to follow a new but equally dogmatic approach.

Yet another magic cure: phonics

The latest panacea is "synthetic phonics". Phonics describes the relationship between letters and sounds, while "synthetic phonics" means building up a word from its separate letters, as opposed to "analytic phonics" – breaking down a word into its letters. The teacher concentrates on a few common letters – typically A, I, N, P, S and T – that make up the largest number of three-letter words. The children pronounce them and join them together to make words.

This technique has some obvious advantages. It is an active method and children quickly get to compose words. Twenty-minute daily doses in the first year at school can be very effective, but disadvantages include the nonsense sentences made up from just these six letters. There is no justification at all for the technique's most fanatical supporters' insistence on abandoning other methods, such as reading for pleasure or making intelligent guesses at a word by using the context. Teaching phonics helps to give beginners confidence, but children need a variety of activities and sensory channels for learning.

Supporters of synthetic phonics have based their claims on an experiment in a few schools in Clackmannanshire, Scotland, involving less than 300 pupils.[4] The children made rapid progress and unexpectedly boys did better than girls. The research showed a lasting impact – at the end of primary school these pupils were about three years ahead of average children. Unfortunately, this was only in single word tests, where children had to decipher and pronounce separate words but not make sense of them. In comprehension tests – complete passages to make sense of – they were only three months ahead.

Distortion occurs when research is based on such artificial tests. If you present words in isolation, children have nothing else to go on but phonics, so it is not surprising if those who have been taught this way do best in this kind of test. Real reading involves a complex mixture of skills: connecting letters to sounds, but also recognising whole words when the spelling doesn't match the sound. How else could we distinguish between "has" and "was", "rough" and "through"? Skilful readers make predictions and don't need to decode every single word. They interpret texts in terms of their own life experience and wider knowledge. They learn to be critical and to spot bias.

When some children start school, they have already enjoyed hundreds of stories and fantastic picture books – they see themselves as readers. We need to give this excitement to all children, through nurseries that are not obsessed with targets, that fully involve parents and lend books to families who can't afford them.

Above all, reading involves learning to make sense of the world. Books carry messages from far away and long ago. They give us new perspectives and experiences. Some books help us deal with complex ideas. Fantasy stories open our minds to lots of possible futures.

Children need a rich education from teachers with real expertise, not mechanical drilling in line with the latest government orders. It is time the government learned to respect teachers, not treat them like robots. Philip Pullman addresses five clear demands to the government:

- Do away with these incessant tests: they only tell you things you don't need to know, and make the children do things they don't need to do.
- Abolish the league tables, which are an abomination.
- Cut class sizes in every school in the country. No class should be bigger than 20.
- Make teaching a profession that the most gifted, the most imaginative, the most well-informed people will clamour to join, and make the job so rewarding that none of them will want to stop teaching until they drop.
- Make this the golden rule, the equivalent of doctors' Hippocratic oath: **Everything we ask a child to do should be worth doing.**

The artificiality of 'literacy'

Pullman's condemnation of artificiality goes to the heart of the matter. The Association of Teachers and Lecturers conducted a survey of English teachers' views on the government's pilot key stage 3 strategy. In my favourite example, one teacher said, "It's almost as if you taught English in a foreign country, as though you are teaching linguistic skills only."

A recent report by Her Majesty's Inspectorate of Education, *Reading for Purpose and Pleasure*, supports the appeal for a change of direction.[5] The inspectors are clearly unhappy at the futility of current advice. They noted:

- Schools seldom built on pupils' own reading interests and the range of reading material they read outside school.
- Although most of the higher attaining pupils read a great deal at home, some did not regard this as learning to read.
- Most schools used books from a range of structured reading schemes as a central resource. Higher attaining pupils...read these quickly and were then able to choose freely from books that particularly appealed to them. In contrast, those who struggled stayed with the scheme for longer. In many schools pupils saw this as something to be worked through until they became a "free reader". One low-attaining pupil commented, "You go up a colour if you're good and down a colour if you're doing rubbish."
- There were still too few suitable books for low-attaining pupils, particularly at key stage 2. The books they were able to read often had an interest level that was well below them:

Really Connecting:

a view from Jim Cummins, an expert on the education of bilingual pupils

Nowhere in this anaemic instructional vision is there room for really connecting at a human level with culturally diverse students. When we frame the universe of discourse only in terms of children's deficits in English and in phonological awareness (or deficits in any other area), we expel culture, language, identity, intellect, and imagination from our image of the child. In contrast...an instructional focus on empowerment, understood as the collaborative creation of power, starts by acknowledging the culture, linguistic, imaginative, and intellectual resources that children bring to school.

Effective citizenship requires active intelligence, critical literacy, and a willingness to challenge power structures that constrict human possibility... Identity, intellect, imagination and power are absent from the new regime of truth because they potentially challenge the smooth operation of coercive power structures.

As the educationalist James Moffett explains:

> Literacy is dangerous and has always been so regarded. It naturally breaks down barriers of time, space and culture. It threatens one's original identity by broadening it through vicarious experiencing and the incorporation of somebody else's hearth and ethos. So we feel profoundly ambiguous about literacy.
>
> Looking at it as a means of transmitting our culture to our children, we give it priority in education, but recognising the threat of its backfiring we make it so tiresome and personally unrewarding that youngsters won't want to do it on their own, which is of course when it becomes dangerous... The net effect of this ambivalence is to give literacy with one hand and take it back with the other, in keeping with our contradictory wish for youngsters to learn to think but only about what we already have in mind for them.[6]

My book just has "Look. Look" in it. (He rolls his eyes.) What use is that? It is too easy.
Year 3 pupil

● She considers herself a good reader "at times" and enjoys reading at home to her mum and dad. She talks of reading books with chapters in them. However, she says that at school she has to read the reading scheme books. They are boring at times but she takes them home and finishes them over a couple of days. However, she is frustrated that she has to wait a week to change the book "because you can only change it on a Tuesday".

The inspectors highlight very different characteristics as the road to success:

Almost all pupils in the most effective schools had some freedom to choose their own books, graded at appropriate reading levels.

They see a place for phonics, but within wider strategies and in short bursts.

There were low expectations in some schools: for example, teachers were not convinced that pupils could learn more than one sound each week.

According to the inspectors, in effective schools "teachers introduced a broad range of reading strategies early on". Pupils are taught to recognise whole words where these are not phonically regular, to use grammar to support comprehension, to make decisions about which strategy will work best (sounding out, skipping a word and reading on, or using context as a cue). While arguing for better resources to interest boys, the HMIs are opposed to narrowly sexist assumptions:

Pupils were rarely consulted about the sorts of books to be included. One boy, a reluctant reader, said of the collections in his school, "They just have sport and science fiction in. I'm not interested in sport and science fiction."

The inspectors insist that pupils make good progress when they see a genuine purpose for their reading. They also complain that reading for understanding is rarely taught across the curriculum – a negative consequence of separating out literacy into its own hour.

Moral panics and reading

The concern about falling standards is not new. It stretches back at least a century.[7] In 1912 a headteacher wrote to the *Times* complaining: "Reading standards are falling because parents no longer read to their children and too much time is spent listening to the gramophone." The 1928 Spens report on secondary education said, "It is a common and grave criticism that many pupils pass through grammar school without acquiring the capacity to express themselves in English."

This panic, which continues to the present day, interconnects with another imagined crisis – of social breakdown and young people out of control – in a general rhetoric about standards. In an interview on the BBC's *Today* programme in 1985, then Conservative minister Norman Tebbit declared:

> If you allow standards to slip to the stage where good English is no better than bad English, where people can turn up filthy and nobody takes any notice of them at school – just as well as turning up clean – all those things tend to cause people to have no standards at all, and once you lose your standards then there's no imperative to stay out of crime.

John Rae, former head of Westminster School, a prestigious private school, has put forward a similar view:

> The overthrow of grammar coincided with the acceptance of the equivalent of creative writing in social behaviour. As nice points of grammar were mockingly dismissed as pedantic and irrelevant, so was punctiliousness in such matters as honesty, responsibility, property, gratitude, apology and so on.[8]

A highly formal version of English teaching, based on analysis and drill rather than understanding and expressing meaning, is seen as the magic cure. There has been a repeated effort to domesticate education, but especially English. In the absence of a detailed syllabus, English once offered the opportunity for speaking, reading and writing on matters of personal interest and social and political concern. The conservative backlash has tried to remove this space by filling it with all kinds of rubble. There is no sane reason why all eight year olds must learn to define assonance and onomatopoeia, but it keeps classes too busy to talk about anything more important.

Opening up the text

We can either read slavishly or critically. We can believe all we see in print, or we can ask ourselves whether conclusions are supported by evidence, and whose side the writer is on. It is the same with advertising, photographs and television.

The Brazilian educationalist Paulo Freire was inspirational for pioneering new ways of teaching literacy, initially with adults in poor rural areas. He began by investigating the words that meant most in local people's lives and built his lessons on them.[9] Decoding letters on the page is never enough – real literacy includes discussing and investigating your own life, its joys and suffering, the causes of oppression and ways of resisting.

This approach to literacy is both grounded and critical. The two go together. Learning to read critically is not just a set of techniques, though they can be learned. It is also a matter of standpoint. This is why some of the most interesting writing has come from people living on the margins of a dominant culture. Working class or Black readers are often able to challenge the views of a respected writer by contrasting the text with their own lived experiences.[10]

The standard technique for developing reading for understanding in British schools, across different ages and subjects, is "comprehension" – an extract from a book followed by questions. Some questions do provoke readers to read between the lines and to evaluate critically what they see, but many simply require repetition or rewording of a chunk of text. It also tends to turn reading into an exercise, even a kind of test.

Many alternatives exist that take the lid off the text, making it seem less authoritative and more open to challenge. In the 1980s a group of London teachers, meeting at the English and Media Centre teachers' centre, developed some practical but powerful ways of opening up texts:

- predicting how a story would continue
- rearranging jumbled paragraphs
- disputing a statement or rewriting it from somebody else's point of view
- comparing two texts on a similar subject[11]

Converting textual information into diagram form can also force the reader to grasp the argument as a whole and help to highlight flaws in the logic. Obviously you have to avoid these methods becoming another set of practice exercises, but a simple repertoire of open and active reading strategies promotes the idea that texts are put together by human beings and that stylistic features produce rhetorical and ideological power.

Critical literacy enables young readers to compare their very different experience of life with an author's views. I was privileged to see 15 year old Asian students working on an episode of the TV drama *Casualty*, which I had viewed uncritically. The episode had two contrasting plots: a white doctor and nurse were in love and getting married, surrounded by family and friends, while an Asian girl and her white boyfriend were pursued by the girl's brother.

The class was able to deconstruct some of the dramatic and filming techniques, initially because the stereotypes had made them angry:

> Khalid the big brother strides in through the dark iron gates and stands there with his cigarette in his hands taking a long puff at it. His eyes look big and round with that look of cool anger burning up inside them. He strides in from darkness to light. This atmosphere was very threatening and menacing. He's got shadows cast upon his face, illuminating and menacing. We as viewers are manipulated straight away that this is the bad guy. The only lights in the tunnel were supplied by the car headlights, but there were strange shadows everywhere.[12]

These students were engaged in media literacy of the best kind, carefully analysing how dramatic techniques along with filming and editing are used to construct stereotypes. At one level it's "just a story" but these students made a very important point: forced marriage has become a popular narrative theme on television, but happily married Muslims never appear, either in dramas or in documentaries.

Introducing contradiction

The initial response of progressive English teachers to the compulsory teaching of Shakespeare in the National Curriculum was to oppose it. The objections were well founded – is Shakespeare sufficiently accessible for 14 year olds in inner city schools? Why allow a play to be destroyed by months of intensive study for the SATs? Despite this, some teachers took a critical stance, using historic texts that raise dilemmas and conflicts with contemporary resonances.

Shakespeare provides rich opportunities for radical teaching. It is easy to produce subversive readings of his works, despite conservative attempts to stick him on a pedestal as an icon of Englishness. Whatever Shakespeare's personal views might have been, his plays reflect the social and ideological turmoil at the birth of the capitalist era. They are so full of negative images of royalty that if he had written political pamphlets rather than drama, he would surely have been executed. Plays such as *The Taming of the Shrew* and *The Merchant of Venice* are criticised for sexism and racism, and Shakespeare often seems to pander to audience prejudice, but these same plays give voice to powerful anti-sexist and anti-racist arguments.

As cultural critic Raymond Williams pointed out, the "heritage" of English literature taught in universities is a selective tradition. The same is true of the school curriculum – it is a selection compiled by those powerful enough to impose their will, on the basis of an established tradition. It can also be shaped in part by the resistance that teachers are able to muster.

The official version of "literature" is a domesticated and depoliticised version. Shelley was the favourite poet of the Chartists, the working class radicals of the mid-19th century, but his most radical poems were left out of school anthologies. Blake's poems were reinterpreted to destroy their radical content. Thomas Hardy's novels, which show the cruel effects of a rural capitalist environment riddled with sexism and moral hypocrisy, were packaged in school editions and study guides as quaint stories about superstitious peasants.

But despite the imposed curriculum, courageous and creative teachers are selecting poems, plays and novels that can arouse engaged and critical debate. The same is true of many other school subjects. Official versions can be subverted and become the source of critical understanding, using "education for citizenship" as a flag of convenience. Since citizenship is a whole school responsibility, teachers can use it to justify a more radical emphasis in the curriculum.

Science and technology lessons can include texts that question the social use and abuse of scientific discovery, looking at the atomic bomb, genetic engineering or antibiotics to promote animal growth, for example. History can compare working class, feminist and anti-imperialist perspectives. Just because Victorian Britain and the Second World War are compulsory topics doesn't mean that we have to teach only the establishment version. Geography raises issues of power in the use of space and resources, for example the seizure of agricultural land in Africa by multinationals and its use for growing cash crops rather than food for the growers. Without undermining enjoyment, all the creative arts can be connected to values and historic change.

Teachers need to be bolder in relating school learning to current events – not as isolated individuals but in cooperation with trusted colleagues. In the last resort, it is unethical and unprofessional to hide behind a fixed syllabus when this fails to deal with the critical issues of the day. The National Curriculum was written before today's quota of 30,000 children died of starvation and before the barbaric occupation of Iraq. We have a duty to our students and to society as a whole not to hide the truth.

Mission critical

Critical literacy can be practised with all ages and in all subjects. Here are some examples from schools in various countries:

Beanie Babies: a class of 10 to 11 year olds discuss the marketing ploys used to sell Beanie Babies soft toys. "He's scaring people into buying them – they want every one of them so he retires them and this makes certain ones more desirable."

A is for Arndale: eight to 10 year olds write an alphabet book on their own neighbourhood, comparing it with commercially published books.

Cooking Afghan-style: recently arrived asylum-seekers in Australia make a video in the style of cookery programmes, but highlighting other cultures. They discover a pocket of 19th century migration from Afghanistan.

The Oregon Trail: a class studies a CD-Rom on the wagon trails across the US Mid West. They discover that women's experiences are completely ignored, and conflict between settlers and Native Americans is presented entirely from a white perspective.

The language of textbooks: students dig behind superficial terminology such as "contact of peoples", deciding on the following terms to classify types of contact – cooperation, exploitation, rejection, mission, forced movement, refuge, resistance.

Museum visit: students visit a museum to ask whose stories are not told there, and then begin to research and set up their own museum. [13]

CHAPTER 8

Curriculum, class and globalisation

A curriculum is not a parcel to be "delivered" but an opportunity to make meaning. Curriculum reform and adaptation are not just a question of modernising, but also a deeply political issue. We are faced with an unprecedented global concentration of wealth and power, and helping young people to understand the big issues of the environment, poverty and war is a matter of life and death.

But the curriculum is being changed for the worse. Opportunities to develop an understanding of environmental and social problems are being removed by New Labour. We are threatened with a lean version of education, stripped down to the bare bones of what employers judge to be useful. The government presents training for work as the only way to make education more relevant and accessible for working class students.

Government ministers speak as if work preparation is the only way to more active and practical learning. But other forms of situation and experience-based learning can also be related to social needs – whether designing a playground (design and technology), measuring the insulation in a council flat (science) or making a video for a local campaign (English).

We need a broad curriculum which engages young people's interests, experience-based activities that will help working class and ethnic minority students to learn, and the right to understand what is going wrong with the world.

The National Curriculum of the 1990s was technologically advanced but socially reactionary. It gave a privileged place to maths, science and technology, which were divorced from ethical and political questions. Broadly speaking, it interpreted literacy and numeracy as technical skills disembedded from authentic use or critical understanding. It attempted to squeeze out opportunities to study current issues and events.

We constantly hear demands that we should go back to basics, but what basic understandings do we need in order to move forwards to a better future? Core skills are important but these are broader than the traditional 3Rs. A curriculum for the 21st century will need to:

- promote concerned understanding and active citizenship
- examine the environmental and social dimensions of science and technology
- challenge the injustice of racism and poverty
- connect mathematics to social issues as well as technical problems,
- develop critical literacy, including the mass media
- raise the status of the creative and performing arts, social development and health

Curriculum and class

There is always confusion when educational writers use the word class. Normally they rely on sociological or official definitions based on occupation and lifestyle. On this basis, the population divides into complex subdivisions such as social classes I to VII, or gradations such as "lower middle class" or "upper working class".

This model can help us understand some educational problems, for example why manual workers' children – usually simply called "working class" – tend to be less successful than others academically, while parents in professional occupations are able to gain educational advantages for their children by helping them to understand school work, by intervening with school problems or simply by discussing academic topics. Examining the reasons for the inequity, and trying to do something about it, is a basic issue of social justice.

We also need to look at a more fundamental definition of class that goes beyond the official social categories: Karl Marx's division of society into capitalists (employers) and wage workers. The vast majority of the population fits the second group, whether in manual or clerical occupations. Most important of all, Marx's concept of class is based on the fundamental conflict of interest between those who own the means of production – factories, offices, land – and those who work for them.

This division between owners and employees makes itself felt every day. The gap has widened between the very rich and the vast majority of employees, not to mention the unemployed. This has led to chronic and widespread poverty – a third of children in Scotland, and half in inner London, are below the official poverty line. But it is not only the poorest and most vulnerable – or manual workers – who are members of a larger working class, if we use a Marxist definition. Clerical and professional workers make up an increasing proportion of trade union membership, while even higher paid jobs can be monotonous or stressful – and generate big profits for the employer. Teachers too belong to the wage workers group – at the most basic level, they sell their skills and are employed to produce a new generation of workers for capital to profit from.

We can see the importance of Marx's concept of class on a global scale. Wealth and power are increasingly concentrated, and a small number of people own most of the planet, while people who used to grow their own food now grow cash crops for international corporations or crowd into shanty towns round large cities in a desperate hunt for work. Capitalism's hold on the world affects the food we eat and the air we breathe. Its drive for oil profits is also the drive to war.

A curriculum that does not tackle these realities is simply failing, however high the test results. Radical teachers need to protect themselves through "balance" – by presenting alternative perspectives – but the traditional practice of avoiding critical perspectives and controversial issues is a denial of social responsibility.

This is not simply the responsibility of geography, history or English specialists, though they have a crucial role. A new publication from the Rethinking Schools network, *Rethinking Mathematics*, provides excellent practical examples of how maths can be based on examples of globalisation and war.[1] Many scientific topics relate to issues of social responsibility. Design and technology can just as easily involve social facilities and environments as individual consumer products. Government ministers speak as if work preparation is the only way to more active and practical learning, but, as we have seen, situated and experiential learning can also be related to social needs.

There is a historic precedent in the 19th century socialists' campaign against "utilitarianism" – the vocationalism of its day. These campaigners demanded "really useful knowledge…concerning our conditions in life, and how to get out of our present troubles".[2]

The problem of abstraction

One of the reasons why manual workers' children tend to experience more difficulty in acquiring school knowledge is its high level of abstraction.[3] Academic language causes problems when teachers fail to connect abstract concepts with everyday language and experiences. This disadvantages students who are not used to hearing academic language at home – the words end up as empty shells rather than meaningful concepts.[4] This does not mean avoiding complex ideas, but we need to find ways into academic language based on rich experience.

The prestige of abstract knowledge and symbols was sanctified in the early 1900s by so-called intelligence tests. Intelligence was assumed to be generic and innate – if this correlated strongly with parental occupation, it was conveniently assumed that manual workers' children were genetically inferior.[5]

As this theory began to collapse, new explanations emerged based on the idea of "language deficit".[6] Some were based on the crude prejudice that certain dialects and accents were inferior. The colloquial speech of working class children was described in quasi-moral terms as bad grammar, slovenly speech, sloppy pronunciation and foul language. Pupils were criticised for "bad grammar" for answering the question, "Where is the squirrel?" with, "In the tree," rather than, "The squirrel is in the tree." Outside school, of course, it is perfectly normal to give short responses without repeating what you have just heard.

The new kind of prejudice emerged in the 1960s as a quasi-scientific explanation for different levels of educational success. "Incomplete" sentences were seen as deficient – and regarded as a working class characteristic or, in the US, characteristic of Black people.[7] Particular dialect forms were described as "illogical" and a barrier to the development of rationality. Examples included the double negative – "I don't want none" – or in African American English, leaving out "is" or "are". There is nothing intrinsically illogical about either form of speech: the first is normal in French, the second in Russian. The use of these forms in Caribbean Creole doesn't make speakers intellectually inferior.

In Britain the linguist Basil Bernstein argued that working class children only used a "restricted code" of speech, while middle class children also used an "elaborated code". Restricted code – for example, using a pronoun rather than a noun – is adequate when you are present in the situation you are describing, but elaborated code – more extended sentences, using nouns – is needed to explain more distant situations. Bernstein argued that close working class relationships encouraged children to rely on restricted codes, and this led to educational failure.

The research was flawed. Children were presented with a cartoon of boys playing football. The middle class pupils explained in elaborated code:

> Three boys are playing football and one boy kicks the ball and it goes through the window. The ball breaks the window and the boys are looking at it and a man comes out and shouts at them because they've broken the window so they run away and then that lady looks out of her window and she tells the boys off.

The "working class" version uses pronouns, assuming that the listener will understand:

> They're playing football and he kicks it and it goes through there. It breaks the window and they're looking at it and he comes out and shouts at them because they've broken it so they run away and then she looks out and she tells them off.[8]

Ironically, the researchers miss the point – the drawing was in front of the children all the time, so pronouns were quite sufficient. The second child simply has a different social understanding of what the situation demands, not a language deficit. (It is also noticeable that the second version is more lively than the first, which is stilted.)

Language deficit theories were received enthusiastically and, in crude popular versions, became a kind of professional folklore. But English has always been enriched by the creativity of working class language, through its local dialects and its exchange with other languages. This works its way into literature and Standard English. Linguistics professor William Labov recorded debates among young Black people on the streets of Harlem, New York, and was able to show how complex intellectual debates about politics and ethics and theology are conducted powerfully in colloquial language. In London educationalist Harold Rosen has exposed another flaw in the language deficit arguments, pointing to the rich verbal culture of politically active working class communities in the London docklands or Yorkshire coalmines.[9]

It is important to help all children to become articulate in formal Standard English and to use academic terminology, but this cannot be achieved unless you show respect for the home language, whether cockney, Creole or Punjabi. Students benefit from moving back and forth between different languages and registers, so they can discuss intriguing situations comfortably with peers before speaking to the teacher and the whole class in Standard English.

A spectrum of symbols and models: linking abstract ideas to experience

The real issue is how best to connect language – and other symbolic forms such as maps, algebra or musical notation – with experience, in ways that restore voice and agency to the learner.

Etienne Wenger, an expert on learning in everyday situations, presents an old Zen problem about knowledge: what does a flower know about being a flower? In one sense, the answer is everything – spreading leaves, absorbing light, soaking up water, budding and blooming – but in another sense, nothing at all.[10] If we ask a flower to teach a science class "it will just stand there, knowing nothing about being a flower, not the first thing".

He then asks a different question: what does a computer know about being a flower? Again, the answer is, everything – and nothing at all. The trouble is, it's a different everything and a different nothing – the opposite. You can type the word "flower" into the encyclopaedia program of your computer and find all the details and definitions, with full-colour images, and let the computer teach your science class. But if – as a reward for teaching the class – you buy your computer a half dozen roses, then the computer will sit there, awaiting some input. It knows nothing.

Wenger argues that human learning requires both participation in an experience and "symbolic representation".[11] Building on this, we can see language and other forms of representation as a spectrum, from the most experiential to the most abstract. For example, a science teacher can build a model electrical circuit, which we can touch, or alternatively use a computerised model. The virtual circuit is more abstract, but it is also more flexible – we can quickly test out the effect of different combinations of bulb and power source. To understand it, however, students may need to relate the image back to the tangible model, which is closer to material reality. Similarly, numbers presented in a familiar context are easier to understand than algebra, which is too abstract, but conversely algebra can help us gain an overview and see the general principles.[12]

We can follow this theme through the work of various writers. Jerome Bruner compared two ways of knowing, narrative (story-telling) and the logico-scientific mode (academic language).[13] Though both are important, the former is under-used in schools, especially with older students. This can disadvantage those who do not have the direct experiences to connect with and interpret the academic explanation. Philip Adey and Michael Shayer argue that scientific learning should begin with rich experience, followed by "cognitive conflict", where the learners find an event puzzling or discordant with previous experience or understanding – and then "construction zone activity", cooperative discussion in small groups.[14] The abstract reasoning depends on the initial experiences, but we can then apply the abstract concepts flexibly to a range of new situations.

We can show this at work in these examples:

- In a science lesson on evolution, groups of 13 year olds designed an island – drawing it, deciding on climate and vegetation. After this concrete preparation, the teacher stimulated "cognitive conflict" by placing the wrong animal on each group's island – a model penguin on a tropical island, a camel in the Antarctic. The groups discussed this excitedly, identifying key physical features of the animal. Working now on large sheets of paper, big enough to show to the rest of the class – a real audience – each group drew an animal and labelled features that were well adapted to an environment: an elephant's thick skin, a penguin's feet.
- In a Bradford primary school, where most of the children were bilingual but with limited English, pupils learned the genre of instructions by writing a recipe. The teacher first demonstrated how to mix the ingredients for a cake, speaking the steps aloud. The children made a cake together, each child performing an action before passing to the next person and speaking each step aloud. These children have to develop spoken English, learn how to read and write, and acquire curriculum knowledge at the same time. The teacher resisted the pressure to rush ahead, insisting on experience and spoken language as the foundation for literacy.
- Simulations open up the complexities of historical situations. Examples include a mock interview for the post of parish priest, designed to examine the power relationships in a medieval society, or family members arguing about which side to support in the civil war, and "hotseating", where someone playing a general or politician is confronted with questions about their conduct.[15]

Arguing that learning needs to be more embedded in real experience does not simply mean immersion in the everyday world. These examples show the benefit of playing at real life. Simulations, play, designing models and using the arts are a kind of "offline" or "off the air" reproduction of reality – they enable us to explore aspects of the real world and at the same time to experiment with alternatives, to imagine things being different.

Simulations offer a bridge between experience and abstract concepts. Dramatic role play, like visual models, creates a kind of imagined world or micro-world. It enables students to move flexibly between narrative and academic language, visual and abstract reasoning. Role play can enable young people to re-examine issues of cultural heritage in a less threatening way, trying on different possibilities and perspectives. They draw on their own knowledge, immerse themselves in a situation, improvise and explore the impact of their ad hoc decisions. They then reflect on this, with the option of repositioning themselves and working out their own values.

Such a process of cultural reflection and repositioning is important because all young people have to deal with deeply embedded ideologies, whether traditional religion or the closed perspectives of a consumerist society. New ways of learning can enable young people to challenge all kinds of oppressive discourse such as sexism, racism, militarism, imperialism and consumerism without their teachers directly telling them what to believe – which in any case is generally futile.

Classroom language and bilingual or working class pupils

The dynamic relationship between experiential and abstract forms of language underlies the work of Jim Cummins, an expert on the education of bilingual pupils. When newcomers are integrated into normal classes, they soon learn the everyday language of conversations and transactions, but academic language takes much longer. Teachers have often mistaken this for a psychological difficulty, and children have been placed in a lower stream or set or in a special school. Even in a mixed-ability class, these pupils are frequently given boring de-contextualised exercises, at a low cognitive level and also low in experience.

Cummins argues that in order to move from "everyday language" (high in experience, low cognitive level) to "academic language" (low on experience, high cognitive level), the intermediate stage should not be decontextualised exercises (low experience and cognition) but activities that are grounded in experience and introduce high-level ideas.[16]

This has considerable relevance to the wider issues about language and working class students – the problem that led Bernstein to his flawed theory of language deficit. Instead of blaming parents for a supposed deficit, we should enrich students' direct experience – and their indirect experience through television and IT. We should help them actively make sense of reality, shifting up and down the spectrum of language and other symbolic representation. This would provide a more solid foundation than the hurried transmission of content favoured by government strategies.

The vocational option

Throughout the Victorian period policy documents openly stated that working class children should not be educated beyond their station in life. In our own times, even when more forward looking employers ask for increased creativity, cooperation and thinking skills, there seem to be unspoken limits on which children will develop these abilities and what they are allowed to think creatively about.

New Labour's Five Year Strategy for Children and Learners – the foundation for subsequent legislation – is in line with this Victorian ideology, and in keeping with the Blairite version of neo-liberalism.[17] Having constantly argued that driving up test scores will attract foreign investment and revitalise the economy, the government is now shifting towards a more direct alignment between schooling and employers' needs – one that divides the school population in two. The five year strategy is a manifesto for increasing control of education by the employing class.

Even a word count is revealing. *Employer* appears 146 times in the strategy, *employment* on 30 occasions and *business* 36 times. The words *creative* and *creativity* appear once each. The word *critical* features six times, but always means *essential* rather than thinking critically or challenging the status quo: "All young people should be equipped with the skills critical for success in employment." There is scarcely a hint that schooling might serve any purpose other than employability.

It is, of course, important for education to prepare young people to make a productive contribution to the economy – whether to earn a wage in a capitalist enterprise or as thoughtful and innovative participants in a future socialist economy. But education has many goals besides this. Schools and colleges should be a space where creativity is developed, where we learn to live together, where we learn empathy and sensitivity towards one another, where young people can reflect on their relationships. Schools – for young people and as learning centres serving the whole community – should be places where we can acquire a cultural heritage and reshape it for our own times, where we can engage in critical thinking about our society and world.

Crucially, in our own times, schools and universities must create opportunities to question and challenge injustice, racism, environmental destruction, militarism, consumerism, the media and political spin. None of this forms any part of New Labour's "vision".

According to the five year strategy, employers will be involved in reforming the curriculum for 11 to 14 year olds. There will be "young apprenticeships" for 14 to 16 year olds; the core curriculum in communication, mathematics and IT for 14 to 19 year olds will be determined by employers; and the next expansion of degree-level education will be "led by businesses", not universities.

Even for 11 year olds, employers will determine what will be taught in English, maths and IT. Many 14 to 16 year olds will be encouraged into "young apprenticeships", spending two days a week in a factory or office. In effect, for the most disadvantaged, the school leaving age is being lowered and these young people will provide several years of unpaid labour.

The number of young people studying after age 16 will increase, but – in the strategy's words – only into "some sort of" education or training. Young people are increasingly expected to continue their education but to pay for it themselves. They are expected – literally – to buy into this way of thinking and invest in themselves as human capital.

When Thatcher's government introduced the National Curriculum, there was at least a broad spread of subjects for all – English, science, geography, art, music, languages, PE. New Labour has eroded this breadth, making many subjects optional, especially for students from poorer families. Increasingly, secondary school will be about training for work.

The 2006 Education and Inspections Bill divides the curriculum, and the school population, into two: a broad range of academic subjects leading to GCSEs, or a vocational diploma. It states categorically that those who opt for the vocational course are no longer entitled to study history or geography, arts or media, design and technology or a foreign language. There is even a parallel version of English, stripped bare of literature or media studies or fiction or personal writing, for the vocational track. It is likely that young people growing up in poverty, including many ethnic minority students, will follow the vocational option. They will be deprived of a broad and balanced education and denied key ways of understanding the world.

Alongside this, even those who pursue the broad academic option will be force-fed knowledge to pass exams. The constant pressure to meet targets will be a distraction from deeper thinking and more exploratory learning. Schools are being redesigned to produce two kinds of citizen: those who know little about the world, and those who have no concern for what they have been taught.

The authors of the five year strategy are forced to admit that many young people are "bored and frustrated". There are many reasons for this: the high levels of poverty, the disciplinarian regime, too few opportunities to show initiative and independence in learning or work cooperatively in groups, and a standardised curriculum that does not allow teachers to take account of young people's interests. None of these is recognised by the government, whose only answer is…preparation for work.

Teaching and learning in secondary schools are in need of reform, because teachers have been encouraged to lecture at classes, drill them with facts for the test, rush to cover the syllabus. In-depth understanding has not been a priority, though many teachers persist in this. Learning needs to be active and engaged. Learners should spend more time outside the classroom, on community-based investigations and visiting interesting places.

The five year strategy sees active and experiential learning exclusively in terms of vocational training. It is not surprising that work skills and vocational courses are appealing to students growing up in poverty and at risk of unemployment and low wages, but it is not enough. A good education should also help young people to understand the causes of poverty and how to challenge the conditions they live in. Though the content and teaching methods need to change, all young people are entitled to understand science and history and the environment, to act, make videos and dance.

CHAPTER 9

What should citizenship classes really look like?

When the National Curriculum was introduced by the Conservatives, "education for citizenship" did not exist as a separate subject. In fact, every attempt was made to prevent schools teaching about present day issues, which were felt to be dangerous territory.[1] Tony Blair's first education secretary, David Blunkett, decided to put this right, in a very limited way, by introducing citizenship as a new subject. It was tokenistic – a "half subject" worth about an hour a week – but it opened up new possibilities for teachers. In fact, it has never been limited to its half-subject status – "education for citizenship" is also a whole-school responsibility, to be conducted through the medium of many other subjects, special events and the general ethos and organisation of the school.[2]

A school curriculum cannot help having some orientation towards citizenship, one way or another. The traditional academic curriculum was essentially suited to transmit the culture and skills of higher social layers – professional and managerial occupations, for example. A vocational curriculum is generally designed to pass on the skills for manual occupations, along with the core skills of functional literacy and numeracy.[3] Academic and vocational curriculums are often geared towards different levels of society. But for all these differences they share the same social orientation – they aim to fit people into society as it is. They see the world as basically static and hierarchically ordered. Preparation for work is more immediate in vocational education, while an academic curriculum provides a longer-term preparation for less well defined duties and roles requiring a range of organisational and cultural skills. The two types of curriculum can sit neatly side by side, though they may be hierarchically differentiated – as with emergent New Labour policy.

Neither a traditional academic curriculum nor a vocational one encourages critical thinking in any radical sense. The academic curriculum provides environmental and social knowledge that can be deployed critically, but presents it as something sacred, as if it were divorced from potential application. A vocational curriculum, on the other hand, is utilitarian, but fixes boundaries so that critical issues do not emerge. Future electricians are rarely encouraged to think about nuclear power, or hairdressers about feminism.

There is a long history of democratic progressive alternatives to both traditional academic and vocational education, based on more hopeful and open-ended visions of humanity. A major influence was the Romanticism movement that arose in Western Europe in late 18th century. This gave rise to progressive theories of education from Rousseau, Montessori, Steiner and others. It emphasised learning by experience, the love of nature, practical experimentation and individual freedom.

An enduring metaphor in progressive education was growth. The educator's role was to support a healthy and natural growth process rather than pouring knowledge into children or training them in industrial skills. Romantic educational thinking had a significant impact on mainstream primary schools in Britain in the 1960s and 1970s, and achieved official recognition in the Plowden Report on primary schools, commissioned by the government in 1967.

An economic downturn and fears that Britain would be uncompetitive provided the impetus for a counter-attack, which has continued to this day – from the speeches of James Callaghan, Labour prime minister from 1976-79, through Thatcher's National Curriculum, to New Labour's proposal for a curriculum controlled by the business world.

But even before the counter-attack a minority of courageous teachers always saw that this kind of progressive reform was inadequate. Progressivism relies essentially on developing a sense of the good, true and beautiful in the individual child. It is largely unpolitical – it fails to understand that the child's development is shaped by power differences and conflicts, and fails to make connections between immediate experiences and the wider forces at work. Australian academic Stephen Kemmis summarised the dilemma when he proposed a socially critical curriculum rather than a liberal-progressive one:

> If changes are to be wrought in our social structure…then individual virtue and individual action will be insufficient to bring them about. They must be brought about by collective action capable of confronting unjust and irrational social structures. The socially-critical orientation sees right knowledge and right action together: it does not value only knowledge and leave action to follow. It therefore requires participation of the school in the life of its community and of the community in the school.[4]

Perhaps Kemmis makes too sharp a distinction between progressive and socially critical education, and the latter can be built on the former. Let us consider some practical examples:

- Primary school teachers frequently introduce the natural world into their classrooms and encourage environmental interests. This can be given critical edge by examining forces that are environmentally destructive in the local area, or by introducing speakers who are involved in environmental campaigns.

- A favourite of many English teachers is the anti-war poetry of 1914-18. This can be connected with historical knowledge of the First World War's causes and of the revolutions that ended it, in order to show that war is not only terrible but can be stopped by collective action. Some teachers are now connecting the poems explicitly to the Iraq war. The video *Dear Mrs Blair*, made by Military Families Against the War campaigner Rose Gentle about the death of her soldier son in Iraq, provides a moving opportunity to relate literature to today's anti-war campaign.[5]
- Many schools responded generously to the appeal to help victims of the 2004 South Asia tsunami with charity collections. Some, such as Filton High School in South Gloucestershire, responded to students' concerns through a cross-curricular inquiry into political as well as natural causes of the disaster.[6]

A very positive example of socially critical teaching grafted on to progressive methods is the work of Chris Searle, a radical English teacher who worked in east London for many years. He encouraged students to write about their direct experiences and the local neighbourhood, but also used this as a launching pad to examine global connections, for example in street names that reflected the British Empire, oral histories and stories of migration.[7]

We need to realise, of course, that there are limits to what a capitalist ruling class will tolerate in educational reform, but we can make spaces for socially critical learning. Clarity of thinking is important so we don't waste our time struggling for a lesser goal. We need to be aware of the subtle censorship that can occur. It is important to keep sight of important dimensions such as:

- a sense of history – that things haven't always been like this, what has caused the change and how things might be different
- a sense of conflict – that there has been resistance, that contradictory forces are at work, that different people see things differently
- a sense of totality – connecting immediate situations to global forces
- a sense of work and human agency – how high culture for some depends on hard work by many, how the world as we know it today is the result of mass economic production, and how we can change the world through our collective action [8]

Almost everything on the curriculum can be connected to citizenship. A good example is Twenty First Century Science, a set of new GCSE courses that highlights the social dimension. Teachers in Hackney, east London, linking science with English and citizenship, have developed challenging resources on "genetics and citizens", which bring out the ideological, political and economic pressures on scientific developments.[9] The Rethinking Schools network, in its latest publication, *Rethinking Mathematics*, has shown how mathematics can draw its examples from current social, political and environmental issues including the Kyoto agreement on climate change, the World Bank and the Iraq war.

Subject divisions

Divisions between curriculum subjects can also block coherent understanding. It is important to discuss how this happens so that we can try to find ways round it. A major breakthrough was made when Raymond Williams and others related English literature to what was happening historically and politically, and to a wider body of political writing. [10] This – and Williams's own working class background – helped him see a class bias in classic texts. He points out, for example, that when Jane Austen writes about visiting one's neighbour, she doesn't mean those living nearest, but a three-mile journey to have tea with someone of equal social standing.

In studying geography, it is common to learn about the existence of poverty in Africa or Latin America but without questioning the causes. We gain an image of the Third World that is fundamentally distorted, since it misses out the dimension of class as an active force. If the curriculum is rigidly divided by subjects, these issues fall outside geography and inside economics, politics or sociology – which are not a part of the standard school curriculum.

The introduction of design and technology was a major breakthrough compared with earlier forms of craft teaching when students simply did as they were told and followed a fixed design. But it is important to recognise that it is based on an individualistic and consumerist notion of the user. It would not be too difficult to move learning forward, for example by designing a public playground or equipment for elderly or disabled people, and to include a broad examination of why such social needs are neglected compared with products for consumer pleasure that can be sold for a profit. The study of technology can also extend to looking at how basic human needs for clean water and housing are fulfilled or thwarted in different parts of the world, in a joint project with geography.

It is difficult for teachers to negotiate common ground within a rigid timetable, but two good examples arose at Filton High School, in response to the tsunami (mentioned above) and the 2005 Make Poverty History campaign. In both cases, the staff agreed they would each teach their subject as timetabled, but use it to provide insights into the main theme. For the tsunami project, the day began and ended with a plenary discussion and presentation for each year group. [11] In many other European countries schools regularly abandon the normal timetable for a "project day" or "project week", often involving events and presentations in the community.

The struggle for democratic learning

Even when there is potentially radical content in the curriculum, it can be undermined by teaching styles that frame knowledge poorly. This is what happens when students have no choice in the topics they study, when there is no opportunity to debate or investigate and when assessment takes the form of testing. Poor forms of assessment can undermine good teaching,

A Curriculum for Global Justice

A group of Scottish school students had no difficulty suggesting how the curriculum could deal with critical issues. Calling themselves Spag8y (Scottish Pupils Against G8 Yobs), they argued that the real yobs are not young people but the G8 leaders and the capitalists who pull their strings.

They are vandals. They make profits out of pumping greenhouse gases into the sky, choking our planet. They destroy rainforests. They bulldoze communities to build unwanted roads. They are greedy and reckless.

They are violent. They sell lethal weapons around the world to make money. They attack people who won't hand over control of their resources, like oil. Bush and Blair started one of the biggest street rammies in history when they invaded Iraq. 100,000 are now dead, and people are still being killed. Nobody slaps an ASBO on them!

They don't care. They pretend to do something about poverty, but they aren't. They go around the globe bullying people into economic deals which make people poor and make the rich richer. They are creating it. They know they are, but they don't care.

Their proposals included:
English: letter writing to heads of state; radical poetry and other literature; writing for public purposes
Maths: debt repayments and interest; redistributing wealth
Science: AIDS, malaria, how a malnourished body functions, greenhouse gases
History: the history of empire and slavery
Religious studies: would God welcome the G8? Should religion have a stronger role in world politics?
Geography: deforestation, urban overcrowding, climate change, land degradation
Philosophy: Debate – does the free market create liberty or destroy it?

as with a GCSE multiple choice test for citizenship. Alternative forms of assessment such as formative feedback, rich tasks and peer assessment are more supportive.[12]

Classroom language in whole-class lessons is dominated by particular patterns of exchange. Even though children ask lots of questions at home, they are quickly socialised at school into never asking questions themselves – other than requests to go to the toilet or use the felt tips. A dominant model is that of "Initiation-Response-Evaluation". The teacher asks a question; a pupil answers; the teacher keeps control by repeating the answer or praising it before starting another round, through another question. There are ways to overcome this, for example by inviting students to discuss a question in pairs or threes and then invite a more considered response. The teacher can also open up discussion following a response, inviting others to comment, or probe an individual's response more deeply through further critical questions.

Another recurrent pattern is for a class discussion to turn into a question and answer session, with the teacher firmly in charge. One alternative is to ask a student to chair. Role play has some advantages over open discussion, as it brings conflicting views and perspectives to the fore. Students find themselves taking up positions and pursuing them to a conclusion, while others feel confident in opposing views from the cover of an assumed role.

Old habits are hard to break and we are often unaware of our deeply ingrained patterns of behaviour. It can help for teachers to have a trusted colleague observe and give feedback, acting as a coach with practical suggestions and encouragement.

Examining some citizenship textbooks, I found these characteristics:

- The student's prior experience was rarely acknowledged.
- Student tasks involved collecting data and some low-level interpretation (a graph, for example) but little opportunity for evaluation, research or critical reading.
- Even seemingly realistic tasks – Why are stereotypical viewpoints dangerous? or preparing a short speech in which you explain why women are under-represented in parliament – were presented as paper exercises for the teacher to mark, rather than opportunities to interact with a real audience.
- Virtually all tasks were intended for individuals, rather than cooperative activities.
- There was little attempt to relate cognitive understanding to feelings or knowledge to action.

All this conveys an implicit code of authority: that knowledge about the world is fixed, certain, objective, unchallengeable, disconnected and sterile. We need to ensure that young people have a sense of voice and agency at school. Let us compare this with the official advice on social education in Denmark:

It can be valuable to work out a plan for the year, so that you can order resources in time and organise guest speakers, but the plan should consist of broad and open possibilities which give room for adjustments and changes, and not least to encourage and accommodate students' participation and co-responsibility.

Learning can start from a theme, which leads through discussion to the formulation of problems and issues. Alternatively, it can arise from questions and issues which students have raised themselves. In this case, the students and teacher need to consider which theme or subject discipline will provide a framework for these issues or problems. In either case, use will be made of some social science methods or concepts.

After discussion in class, students decide on topics for individual or small group research. These are then presented back to the whole class, but this is more than just a report-back or summary – it is the occasion for further debate:

In the final stage, the results may take the form of reports, folders, posters, etc. but they are not always a physical product. The students might produce their results as a talk, a drama or a simulation game, leading to discussion. This stage has great importance and is not just a closure to the learning process. The learners should be clear that they may not be able to reach final conclusions, but only provisional answers. The final stage also involves an evaluation by students and the teacher of the entire learning process. [13]

Dealing with controversial issues

Avoiding controversy is a deeply ingrained characteristic of British educational culture. Nervous of introducing controversial issues, many teachers unconsciously tend either to avoid them altogether or to steer a neutral middle ground. Good teachers are naturally wary of abusing their authority, but there are other ways to deal with debatable topics without sanitising them. A teachers' conference in Germany presented an alternative code of practice:

- You must not overpower. It is unethical to take pupils unawares, however that is done, in imposing preferred opinions and thus to prevent learners reaching an independent judgement.
- Whatever is controversial in social science and in politics must openly appear controversial in teaching.
- Pupils must be placed in a position where they can analyse a political situation and their own interests and position, and also look for ways of influencing it. [14]

There are many ways to deal with controversy that avoid overpowering or abusing authority and make different viewpoints visible and open to critique, including role play and "hot-seating". The hot-seating technique was developed for studying literature or drama: the person playing Lady Macbeth, for example, sits in the middle of the group and is confronted with questions about her actions and emotions. These can come either from the audience or from students playing other roles. Hot-seating can be adapted to real-life issues, for example:

- A student playing the role of Tony Blair or George W Bush could be asked to justify their decision to invade Iraq.
- An abstract concept can be put in the hot seat, such as imperialism or, more concretely, the British Empire in the 19th century or the US today.

Both these situations could be enhanced by the other students speaking in role, or by the teacher providing a provocative short text, such as South African Archbishop Desmond Tutu's summary of colonisation:

> When the missionaries first came to Africa, they had Bibles and we had the land. They said, "Let us pray". We closed our eyes. When we opened them, we had the Bibles and they had the land.

It is possible to radicalise compulsory topics, even within the constraints of a standardised curriculum. A study of ancient Rome can be connected with US domination of the world today. A US teacher has described how, instead of extensive lectures on Roman civilisation, they challenged students to investigate the question, "Were the Romans civilised?"

It is important to make contradictory viewpoints visible – to constantly raise the questions of whether everybody sees things in a particular way or whether a writer's ideas relate to social position, class, race or gender. Again this can be done through role play.

I ran a workshop at an international conference in Macedonia attended by teachers and school students from all the Balkan countries and different parts of the US. They planned to continue working together through an electronic link up.

- Each group attempted to write a code of rights – similar to the United Nations Declaration of the Rights of the Child – for a specific social group such as teenage girls, elderly people, religious minorities or parents of young children. This led to more focused thinking than memorisation of the standard lists of human rights or even open discussion. (Some of the Americans were amazed to learn for the first time, from a Rumanian participant, about paid maternity leave.)
- As a form of feedback, we simulated a parliament or assembly, in which each interest group sought to convince the others to include five points in a general code of rights. This led to engaged debate, some compromise and amendment, bringing out the need to justify a position.
- In an evaluation at the end of the workshop, there were many suggestions for ways to develop a greater sense of agency – for example, by taking the campaign into the public arena, making posters or approaching local politicians.

More open architectures for school learning

Too much traditional school learning has been a form of alienated labour, rather like factory work:

- You are told what to do.
- You are told how long to do it for.
- You hand over the product, not to a real user or audience but to the teacher.
- In exchange, the teacher gives back a mark – a kind of surrogate wage.

Again learning seems to have an *exchange value*, never a *use value*.

The reward becomes increasingly meaningless as students grow older – neither stickers nor merit certificates will buy the things they want, so why not put their efforts into their paper round? This emphasis on extrinsic rewards as an incentive to improving results needs to be supplemented, if not replaced, by a transformation of school work so that it becomes intrinsically rewarding, with students writing for a real audience – even if this is just the rest of the class – or for publication, or presenting ideas on a real problem to people who are genuinely looking for an answer.

Recent government reforms have established a tight discipline over learning, dividing lessons into three or four short parts, all carried through to a pre-arranged plan and at rapid pace. More open architectures for learning involve a shift of focus from the single one-hour lesson to longer periods of time. Three methods that can create spaces for students to exercise their voice and agency, which involve decision making and a real audience, and could lead to real and significant outcomes, are discussed below.

(1) The project method

The project method was developed by educationalists W H Kirkpatrick and John Dewey, and commonly practised in Northern Europe. The Danish guidance on social education cited above follows this method. The project begins with a theme or issue introduced by the teacher or pupils. This is discussed freely and critically, so ideas and questions emerge.

The next stage is independent research or enquiry, with each group or individual student choosing to investigate a particular aspect. In the final plenary stage, each group presents to the class and stimulates further debate. Where possible, there is a fifth stage, involving a real-world outcome.

(2) Storyline

Storyline is a form of thematic work structured by a narrative.[15] This can be based on a novel, but more often the bare outline of a story forms the skeleton. This method also gives scope for independence within a community of learning. It begins with a situation or location; then participants invent characters for themselves – hotel staff or families in a town, for example. The teacher – perhaps playing the role of postal worker, politician or television news reader – moves the story forward by announcing an event. Each such event is the stimulus for research, fictional or formal writing, improvised drama, art or discussion. Although the method was invented in Scotland for young children, it is used to age 18 in Scandinavia.

Some Scottish teachers have developed a storyline based on the Viking invasions. It starts with pupils painting a mural of a bay, but it is empty – just sea and sand and hills. They then invent characters for themselves, to act in these roles. They research houses of 1,000 years ago, after researching in books and on the internet, and each family paints the house it imagines itself living in and places it around the bay. One day they arrive at school to find a ship in the bay, which some guess is a Viking ship. Some time later in the storyline, they arrive to find the ship missing and a life-size figure of a Viking warrior on the wall. The pupils launch into a big political debate in which the pupils as villagers confront the Viking for what his friends have done. A storyline such as this could also be used to begin a study of imperial conquest.

(3) Design challenges

"Design challenges" present problems that involve investigation and lead to creative solutions, which are presented to an audience.[16] One such challenge, run over two days during pupils' first month at a secondary school, involved core learning skills – using the library and IT-based research, spoken and written communication, Powerpoint presentations, small group cooperation and planning – as well as geographical and scientific knowledge. It began with a video message from "the Emperor of the Galaxy" about his plan to build a superhighway across space from the "capital" to a new holiday resort. Unfortunately, the emperor's plan meant destroying the earth. The earthlings' challenge was to prove that the world was worth saving.

These various methods provide spaces for learning communities to develop, for engaged learning that is critical and creative and connected to real life, for a new relationship between experiential involvement and symbolic representation in a range of media, and the exercise of voice and agency.

They provide possibilities for engaging students from marginalised communities, overcoming their feelings of low status and powerlessness. They provide a broader and richer means than vocational training to engage in learning that is active and feels relevant. They help bridge the gap that worried the linguist Basil Bernstein, between language embedded in immediate experience and more abstract theoretical registers. They provide, in their different ways, for both narrative and academic language.

These new techniques are much more frequently used in many other European countries – some examples are described in the appendix. Scotland's new "Curriculum for Excellence" will also open up diverse possibilities by reducing the amount of content that has to be covered. It is more difficult in England's tightly regulated school environment, but ingenious teachers will find a way.

The refugee project

Student teachers in Edinburgh use Project Method in order to understand issues relating to asylum seekers.

It begins with a simulation based on a mythical future: a military coup in Scotland. Grouped into families, they react to news broadcasts. At one point a member of each family has to go into hiding. Eventually conditions become so bad that the whole family has to flee, but where to? And what happens when they arrive at their destination?

Then two students are asked to act out an interview based on the true experience of a refugee from Afghanistan. He had been asked a series of questions to test whether he really came from that country. The students found it impossible to answer questions on which Scottish newspaper had the biggest circulation or what was the longest river.

The discussion that follows generates many different sub-topics for further research. Different groups opt to investigate factual questions – reasons for flight, countries of origin, regulations, maintenance; or ideological ones – the nature of national identity, attitudes to migration, moral responsibility, xenophobia and racism.

Finally, each research group teaches the rest, including activities to stimulate further discussion. Some groups choose to continue with the topics later during the year.

A storyline from Norway:

Pupils at Ringstabekk School, Norway, described how they worked through a *storyline*:

Rainbow Street doesn't really exist. It's the framework for a storyline. That's a way of working in which pupils work their way into roles as fictional people in a convincing situation. Often we form family groups, and the teachers set up events.

We first had to decide the number of people in each family, our sex and age and religion, our jobs and interests, and we drew the houses we would live in. Rainbow Street is meant to be in East Oslo, and represents life in a multicultural society.

We had arrived at school to see that somebody had written on the houses and synagogue in Rainbow Street: "Norway for Norwegians", "Hitler was right" and "Muslims are parasites". It was a cold November morning. The street's inhabitants were horrified – "What's happened?" "Who can have done something like that?" – There were strong reactions of mistrust between the families in the following days.

The preacher

One day those of us playing children were ordered into a classroom for a special visitor. One of our teachers was dressed as a preacher. He had a Bible, and asked us our religion. He scowled when anybody said Muslim, Jewish or Hindu. He idolised the Christian god and everything to do with Christianity. We were frightened. He was a real fire and brimstone preacher. When he left, each family met to discuss what had happened. There was uproar – isn't there meant to be religious freedom in Norway? We saw all religions as of equal value.

The Klugheim family

One day we were told that the Klugheims had moved into the empty house. They seemed intolerant. Two brothers, refugees from Iran, applied to convert the second floor of their house into a small mosque, including permission for a call to prayer. The Klugheims sent a protest letter.

A meeting took place. The Muslims felt undervalued and oppressed. Some of the other families felt the call to prayer would be a disturbance, but after discussion realised that their objections were less important than its value for the Muslims, and it wouldn't be very loud. We later found graffiti on some of our houses. The Klugheim children were our main suspects, but we couldn't get to the bottom of it.

A visit to Oslo

We visited the International Cultural Centre and Museum to see an exhibition of immigration to Norway since 1945. Twenty people's life stories were on display, with pictures and personal effects. Then Anita from the Organisation against Public Discrimination spoke to us about religion, culture, migration and racism/discrimination. We visited the synagogue, and a lady spoke to us about her conversion to Judaism. We had so many questions. It helped us to prepare for some writing about religion and personal orientation.

Storyline has helped us understand tolerance, discrimination and racism through experiences – in role, some of us had faced antagonism because of the colour of our skin or our culture. It was much more effective than if we'd sat and listened to the teacher talking all the time. We have a much better sense of living in a multicultural society.

CHAPTER 10

Conclusion: Resistance and renewal

Our schools today are the result of a complex struggle. On the one hand, we have an endless torrent of initiatives from the government – acting more and more overtly on behalf of business. On the other, we have the teaching profession and its allies, especially parents. Though weaker than in the 1960s and 1970s, teachers have exerted considerable resistance and pressure through the NUT and other unions, and in different ways through curriculum organisations.

At particular times these forces have combined in campaigns such as the Anti-SATs Alliance and the emerging struggle against city academies and trust schools. The Rethinking Education network aims to build such an alliance, combining public criticism of damaging government policies with the capacity to share more radical ideas and classroom resources.

Alongside struggles over teachers' pay and working conditions, the campaign against national testing has been particularly significant. This focus is crucial, since the test regime has a pervasive influence on the curriculum, teaching and learning, and school life in general. This is, as we have seen, "high-stakes testing" – its impact extends far beyond the initial purpose of measuring learners' attainment.

SATs have never been popular with classroom teachers. Even the moderate ATL teaching union wrote to its members in 2003:

> We believe the government is neglecting the professional expertise that teachers can offer through the assessment process. Our members have deep concern about many aspects of the national curriculum assessment. There is an opportunity for the department to make real progress but only if it can engage the teaching profession in an open and constructive dialogue.[1]

The plain fact is that neither New Labour nor its Tory predecessors have ever had any real intention of involving the teaching profession in their decision making. As early as 1976 the Labour prime minister, Jim Callaghan, spoke of his determination to open up what he claimed to be the "secret garden" of the school curriculum and make schools and teachers more "accountable" to parents and the public. After a constant barrage of orders, initiatives and strategies – sometimes accompanied by phoney consultation exercises – any idea that politicians would seriously consult the workers who run the schools is fanciful.

So how has the teaching profession allowed itself to be bullied into the position where SATs, league tables, comparative test data and performance related pay have become central to teachers' working lives?

The first thing to emphasise is that between 1990, when the first key stage 1 SATs were piloted, and 1995, when tests at key stages 1 to 3 had been fully implemented, the battle between teachers and the government was fierce. Early SATs pilots were either abandoned or ignored as inconclusive because of opposition from the teaching profession, despite the government's efforts and its use of financial incentives for teachers.

Faced with this non-compliance, the government bought time by promising a full review of the National Curriculum. Meanwhile, it exploited the perennial weakness of the teaching profession – the rivalry between different unions – by addressing the chief concern of one of the unions, the NASUWT: workload.

The NASUWT always argued that its opposition to SATs was based on the increased workload imposed on its members. The NUT's action was based on broader educational principles. The government managed to appease the NASUWT by employing external markers – whose incompetence has undermined the reliability of the tests ever since – and by characterising the NUT's opposition as purely political. During the ensuing arguments over legality and political motivation, the NUT was left isolated and the testing regime quickly established itself.

SATs became part of the educational furniture. Even though the government succeeded in imposing its will, SATs remain as unpopular as ever – and not only with teachers. Phil Willis, the Liberal Democrat education spokesperson, has identified the spiralling cost:

> There has been an explosion in spending on producing league tables. Spending 97 percent more on them than in 1997 is misguided when so many schools are suffering budget cuts. I'm sure that most schools and parents could think of better ways to spend £30 million.[2]

The 2001-02 annual report of the Chief Inspector of Schools said:

> The drive to improve performance in national tests in English and mathematics also absorbs more teaching time, particularly in Years 2 and 6. Headteachers report that, when something has to give, it is often extended practical or problem solving activities in subjects such as science, technology and art that are squeezed out. This represents a serious narrowing of the curriculum.[3]

This was nothing more than a reflection and articulation of what most teachers and parents knew.

It gradually became clear that little was changing under the New Labour government, with its various Strategies that further reduce teachers' professional control, and abusive attacks on comprehensive education. SATs became an issue once again.

On the back of growing disquiet in schools and consistent campaigning by NUT activists, the Anti-SATs Alliance was established at a conference in London in June 2003. Comprising parents, teachers and governors, the alliance campaigned vigorously in schools and among parents for the abolition of SATs; 12,000 copies of the booklet *Why We Must Stop the SATs* were sold.[4]

Children's writers including Philip Pullman, Michael Morpurgo and Beverley Naidoo threw their weight behind the campaign – and author Pat Thomson entertained many a public meeting with the story of how she answered a SATs paper based on a passage of her own writing and failed it. Stalls in town centres, meetings with parents and surveys among teachers showed that SATs remained as unpopular as ever. In the autumn of 2003 the NUT took the lead and organised a ballot for a full-scale campaign of industrial action – the boycott of primary school tests.

The ballot result was overwhelming but unsatisfactory. Over 80 percent of those who voted were in favour of a boycott, but the turnout – at just over 28 percent – did little to convince the NUT leadership that concerted, successful industrial action was a possibility (although this will be easier in future, under a new union rule).

Activists who had been central to the ballot campaign and battled vigorously for a positive vote were now faced with a dilemma – one that required close analysis. Could it possibly be that, despite their reservations about the tests and how they affected the curriculum, many teachers had grown reliant on a system that they knew to be "safe"?

In an era of league tables, performance related pay and short-term contracts, it would hardly be surprising if, even against their better judgement, many teachers felt that it was better to "play the game". How easy was it for a young or inexperienced teacher to challenge the prevailing orthodoxy if that was constantly reinforced in their school? And if all you'd ever known in your teaching life and training was the straitjacket of tests, booster classes and constant target-setting, how might a teacher visualise life without these guidelines?

It became clear that a wider debate was needed, and that union and public campaigns must be reinforced by a critical discussion of what was happening to education.

The picture is not all negative. We all know of innovative and experimental practice that is taking place in schools. There is scope for creativity and fun despite the unwarranted level of prescription. Ironically, in those places where teachers have taken liberties, the only impact on test results has been beneficial. The job of activists includes demonstrating that teachers are perfectly capable of running the curriculum by themselves and of breaking free of the repetitive, mind-numbing tedium of the government Strategies and their associated methodology.

Government intervention in education since the mid-1980s has been overwhelmingly reactionary. It has undermined much of the enlightened practice developed in the preceding decades. But it has never completely eliminated it. Despite exhaustingly bureaucratic requirements from government and fear of breaking the rules, teachers continue to develop exciting approaches to learning. Many innovative resources have been published by groups of teachers working together in a variety of organisations, including:

- curriculum associations such as the Association for Science Education and the United Kingdom Literacy Association
- the English and Media Centre, still running nearly 20 years after being officially closed down.[5]
- the regional Development Education Centres
- charities and campaigning organisations such as Christian Aid and Greenpeace[6]

Inspired by the success of Rethinking Schools in the US, campaigners organising in Rethinking Education here are aiming to build a practical alternative to the thin, measly fare of approved textbooks, practice papers and repetitive exercises.[7]

The central mission of Rethinking Education is to combine campaigns about government policies with the sharing of practical classroom ideas. The struggle for a democratic and engaged education needs to unite both these strands. The current campaign against academies, for example, is strengthened by showing better ways to develop successful urban schools with an interesting curriculum. The embarrassing failure of the academies even to deliver the government's agenda calls for a new direction for educational change.

Activists and campaigners know that there is a wealth of material and resources out there – in the hands of classroom teachers – all of which can contribute to a lively and progressive curriculum. Despite the worst efforts of the politicians during the last decades, the ideological battle for a worthwhile education is far from over.

At the time of writing, a thoughtful and vocal campaign is under way against the Education and Inspections Bill. Even if it does become law, this opposition will have laid the foundation for countless local battles to stop businessmen and religious cranks seizing control of state-funded schools.

The curriculum struggle has taken on a new importance when defending schools against neo-liberal policies. Young people should not be forced to choose between vocational certificates and a broad and varied curriculum. We must assert their right to study drama and science and history and languages and the mass media, and to learn how to think for themselves.

Sociologists speak of periods of *settlement* when tension and struggles give way to a working agreement on how to proceed – a kind of truce between different interest groups. Despite the pervasive spin of governments, conveying the impression that there is no other way to run schools, education is extremely unsettled at present. The precise conditions and issues change, but the essential problem remains that outlined in this book's opening chapter: a ruling class that needs workers who are clever enough to be profitable but not wise enough to know what's really going on. It is our task to make sure that young people are able to gain the knowledge and motivation to change life for the better.

We must overcome the deep pessimism and fatalism that hang over education today. There are enormous obstacles, but perhaps the greatest is our own fearfulness. Another world is possible. Another school is possible, and will help us to heal a sick world. The relentless drive for higher test scores matters far less than caring and creative learners, a sense of justice, a world at peace, our common welfare and the future of our planet and all its people.

APPENDIX

Other places, other schools

Two case studies of very innovative schools – one in Germany, the other in Spain – offer inspiring examples of what can be achieved.

Case study one: The Laborschule, Germany

The Laborschule – or laboratory-school – in the city of Bielefeld is one of a handful of "experimental schools" in Germany, and undoubtedly the most influential. The brainchild of Hartmut von Hentig, a radical education professor at Bielefeld's new university, it was set up in 1974 as a curriculum laboratory like John Dewey's Laboratory School in Chicago – a place where new ways of teaching could develop and be evaluated, and then spread into the mainstream system. For three decades the Bielefeld school has provided a warm and stimulating environment for children to learn and grow up in. It has hundreds of visitors a year and has had enormous influence on schools in Germany and internationally.

The school runs across the primary and secondary age range, from age five to 16. Children normally enter a year before compulsory schooling begins and stay for 11 years. After that all routes are open, including the final stage of the traditional Gymnasium (grammar school) or the Oberstufenkolleg (sixth-form college) next door. The Oberstufenkolleg is another von Hentig creation, with similar developmental aims, and provides a unique pre-university curriculum. The Laborschule is fully comprehensive, and admissions are controlled to reflect the social profile of the city's population.

In 2002 the Laborschule made national headlines, following the OECD's shock findings about educational standards in Germany. At the request of researchers, and after months of debate, Laborschule teachers agreed that its pupils would sit the tests used in the OECD's PISA study elsewhere. This was a daring step, as the Laborschule's curriculum is radically different and its ethos is not "academic" in any narrow sense.

The results were amazing. After careful matching, using parental occupation and educational details, its pupils were found to be easily on a par in academic standards with those at the elite Gymnasium. The less advantaged pupils achieved much higher results than their comparators at the Hauptschule – the equivalent of a secondary modern in England. The researchers also looked at social attitudes and political understanding – central to the Laborschule's vision – with highly positive results.

A morning in House One

The 180 infants, in their open-plan House One building, are in mixed-age classes as a matter of principle. Socially and educationally, the school recognises that children develop in different ways and at different rates. It provides social groups in which children learn to take care of one another. Within each class children also belong to mixed-age family size groups of five, with the older ones helping to look after newcomers. It is a positive advantage in learning to read, write and work with numbers – the children help one another as much as they are helped by the teacher.

At the end of their third year the children leave these mixed-age groups to join the age-based class where they will stay for the next eight years. There is a ritual in which each child carries a sunflower into their new class, to signify growing – echoing a similar event when they first joined the school.

I spent a great morning with Eva's class of five to eight year olds. Children started arriving from 8am, and settled down to activities of their choice. Some read, some played board games on the carpet, and some chatted with their teacher or with each other. At 8.30am we sat in a circle on the floor, with one new child almost in Eva's lap. All the children were excited about yesterday's show: they had presented a shadow theatre for their parents, and were able to see it on video.

The class had seen modern paintings in an art gallery, and re-presented them through mime. The show was very funny as three of the boys, acting the part of art gallery staff, emerged from time to time to clown with the audience, dusting them as well as the pictures. We went round the circle – every child began, "What I found great about yesterday was..." before the group moved into open discussion. There was also time to discuss the activities that various children wished to pursue later in the morning.

The next part of the day, from 9am, was devoted to language and maths. It was individualised, and each child knew what to do. Some were working alone, others in pairs – acting cooperatively or tutoring each other. Some worked on arithmetic, others on reading or writing, with some using textbooks, and others games or equipment. The teacher had plenty of time to help particular children read. I was worried about one child who didn't seem to settle. Eva, who has been at the school many years, reassured me: he's got some family problems – he will settle, and he will learn to read before long, everyone does.

Next came second breakfast – a birthday party today with cakes and drinks as well as sandwiches. Easy and relaxed, this was an important social event. Three boys took their turn to wash up, while the others went outside or stayed in for break – their choice. Some children returned to board games, others to play outside. Others watched the gardener and older children laying out a new flowerbed.

Break and lunchtime at the Laborschule are important learning times, though not directed by the teacher.

The time between break and lunchtime can be used in various ways, including learning about the world and creative arts. There is no fixed curriculum – "Isn't this what you do in England? We've learnt a lot from English primary schools." It had been a long time since Eva's visit.

Sometimes a project is shared with other classes, ending with a performance. Most learning is experiential. Von Hentig's famous motto applies: "As far as possible, we should replace instruction with experience," although we mustn't forget the other half of his dialectic: "The teacher's role is to bring experience into consciousness."

School lasts all day for the older pupils but this is thought to be too long for the infants. Some children go home at lunchtime, but others stay to be looked after by other staff in the afternoon with activities, play and visits.

The school buildings

The Laborschule's main building consists largely of open-plan areas where each class has a home base. Much of the learning takes place here, and the children learn a special courtesy for each other. There is little noise or interference. At one end, outside the headteacher's and secretary's rooms, there is a coffee area where teachers sit and talk, sometimes joined by older students. However this main building and its grounds also have plenty of specialist areas: science labs, a library and workshops, as we might expect; but there is also the "zoo", the school garden, a disco, media room, kitchen and so on.

The oldest students have recently moved into a new area, well equipped with computers. What did I think of it? "Lots of potential, but it seems a bit bare, as if the students haven't really taken ownership of it yet." I was told they were planning a *project week* devoted to the school environment, during which creative and technical skills would be developed – making room dividers, house plants, mosaics.

The library is spacious and provides extensive resources for individual and class use. The zoo? Well, it's not exactly tigers, but pets that the children contract to take care of, at school or at home – an important way of learning responsibility. The school garden is an important learning space, where many pupils have their own plots. There is a playground built by the children, a maze, and pupils also run the *disco* – a social area – with help from a community worker. The sports halls are shared with the sixth form college. All these specialist spaces are used informally during the break and lunchtime, and also for relevant courses – there is a thin boundary between formal and informal learning.

Learning frequently happens off the school premises. For example, building the maze involved lessons from bricklayers and visits to building sites. There is a class visit, lasting at least a week each year, in which children learn to cook and look after themselves. A work experience placement occurs in each of the three senior years.

The curriculum

The Laborschule's curriculum has evolved over time. It is not tied to normal government requirements of subject provision but instead results from well planned experiments, which are carefully evaluated for pupil motivation and effectiveness. Currently, for example, there is a pilot mixed-age class for eight to ten year olds and well established mixed-age options for 10 to 13 year olds.

Surprisingly, given their success in the OECD tests, pupils in this age range are not taught German language and literature as a separate subject – it is entirely integrated into other learning. Some integration is also evident for older students, and classes frequently have the same teacher for German and integrated humanities (history, geography, citizenship).

Assessment

The Laborschule is a school where marks and grades are banned. Well, almost: the exception is the final year, when grades are required for admission to the next stage of education in other institutions. Until then, they are replaced by formative feedback, including peer evaluation – children learn to be supportive but also helpfully critical. Reports take the form of a letter to the child, highlighting strengths and weaknesses and recommending future action. Great care is taken with the tone of these communications – they regard nothing as fixed, especially not personal characteristics, and avoid being judgemental:

> Dear Sebastian [age six]
> Do you know, I always look forward to seeing you in the morning. Even during circle time, you're so attentive, and then in the Learning Time [literacy/numeracy, infants] you work conscientiously, carefully and quite independently – and for a whole hour. It's not surprising you're making so much progress in maths...

> Dear Marcel [age 13]
> I'm worried that you're still not achieving the goals of our science course. You hold back too much in discussions, and there are gaps in your written tasks. You're a lot better with practical work. The senses touch-box you made was a great success. I hope you'll concentrate harder next year, as it's a demanding course – I know you can.

Experiential learning

There is an emphasis on projects with practical outcomes, as a vehicle for learning. Examples include a circus production, public reading of folk tales written by the pupils, film-making, selling a product and eco-gardening. Some projects are on a bigger scale, involving one or more year groups, for example a project on "Life in the Middle Ages". Some involve international cooperation – there is a long-standing link with Nicaragua and a UNESCO project with a Swedish partner. Decision making and project planning by the students is very important, with sufficient choice over activities and outcomes. Results such as exhibitions, performances and products are a way of sharing with the school community, parents and often the wider community – and an important motivator.

The Laborschule gives new meaning to the *learning community*. In planning the curriculum, emphasis is placed on the relationship between "hand, heart and mind" – in line with the Montessori educational theory – and on social responsibility. There is an emphasis on curriculum as a process – von Hentig proposed that in their early years, children should:

- pursue an interest together, show each other, talk about it
- step back from the group – be alone
- literally explore the elements – make a fire, dam water, dig a hole
- build a hut, plant a garden or look after an animal
- cook together and eat it – wash up afterwards
- read quietly
- observe something, observe others, follow your curiosity
- celebrate special occasions, perform something, sing, give each other presents that they have made themselves
- and all of that alongside the normal school activities – writing, reading, calculating, drawing, cleaning up

Gender

One development project focuses on gender equality at the school. Some girls asked for a space where they could discuss issues with teachers without boys around. A central concept is that girls, who mature earlier than boys, enjoy the experience of their physical development, but it is both a means of pleasing others and a potential risk. The project created a space not only for girls' health and sex education, but also for aesthetic and emotional experiences related to their bodies, through dance, drama, psychodrama, art, music, self-defence and relaxation. The girls created physical environments with candles, flowers, etc, and developed a code of practice, in particular not carrying people's personal stories outside the group. They also engaged in role-play to develop assertiveness.

The boys then insisted on their own course. Teachers have developed this on the principle of reflective rather than anti-sexist boys' work. They wanted to avoid falling into a "deficit" or blame model, though an important focus is boys' behaviour as a group, and towards girls. Pupils' suggestions also resulted in a housekeeping certificate based on skills acquired on a residential; and a very popular placement during which teenage boys care for young children in nursery schools and playgroups.

The leavers' year

Christoph teaches a final year class for German and humanities, and is also their form teacher. When I arrived in his class, the students were just finishing a unit on the resistance to fascism. Individuals and groups had researched a choice of topics and each group made a presentation to the class. They had clearly used some very challenging resources, including books originally written for adult students. During each presentation the rest of the class listened carefully, discussing how a particular form of anti-fascist resistance might have had greater impact, why more hadn't taken part and how that would have helped.

They collectively evaluated the work – a positive appraisal, with suggestions for improvement next time. This theme linked history, citizenship and literature. School learning also connected with citizenship in the real world: many pupils had recently joined university students and members of the public in protests when conservative politicians tried to stop an exhibition showing the German army's complicity in the Holocaust during its occupation of Eastern Europe.

In another of Christoph's lessons, they were writing about dream towns. This was a creative writing activity in which pupils – drawing on personal interest in sport or the environment, for example – designed a new town. This connected with their geography curriculum – looking at maps and photographs of the centre of Berlin, which was then being rebuilt. This unit linked together descriptive, analytic, moral and imaginative processes, and various forms of communication – factual and creative writing, maps and photos.

As an informed visitor, I asked myself how I would know if the quality of literacy was high enough. There are differences between German and English language – for example, German spelling is less of a problem, but the sentence structure of formal German is elaborate. I was surprised that even the two boys who wrote least were forming complex academic sentences quite accurately. Perhaps the quality and extent of discussion and formal presentations form the basis for academic literacy.

Towards the end of the lesson a group of girls in another class returned unexpectedly early from their science lesson. I wandered over. Why had they come back early? They had finished an ambitious activity, rewriting a text about energy – enzymes, food, photosynthesis – more simply. What were they discussing now? I had expected them to say boys, pop stars, clothes. In fact, they were chatting to one another about their extended individual studies: one about Jamaica, one on dolphins, one comparing acting in theatre and film. One was studying Che Guevara, another Freud and Jung's theory of dreams. Two students had produced exhibitions rather than folders: one a thematic display of her poems and stories, with illustrations, the other a set of costume designs, displayed in the building's main corridor. The school is committed to mixed-ability teaching, but this does not place a ceiling on anyone's learning.

Every teacher in the school supervises a small number of final year projects, according to their particular interests. I overheard a discussion between the deputy head, Annemarie, and a student who had been studying American Indians – a comparison of two different cultures and their near extermination by white settlers. The student had produced an impressive folder, both conceptually and in its visual presentation – a source of pride. Other students had been studying the Celts, whether ethics depends on religion, and alternative versions of Snow White.

School development
What kind of processes sustain the Laborschule's development? Are these different from elsewhere? Headteacher Susanne Thurn gave me some pointers, before rushing off to speak at a conference – a universal problem: headteachers in a hurry.

- An important issue is the school's commitment to self-evaluation, supported by critical friends. The school is not subject to external inspection, but works closely with the regional staff development institute and chooses its own external advisers to support and evaluate developments. As well as a head and deputies, the school has a university professor as its academic adviser.
- Teachers volunteer to lead development projects, for which they are released from some teaching. These projects often involve cooperation with the university, the publication of new resources and careful evaluation.
- Individual development is vitally important. There is a weekly meeting for new staff. The school naturally appoints teachers who are committed to its philosophy and practices – and there is no shortage of applicants – but there is inevitably a cultural shift when they come from other schools, and some newcomers find the transition difficult and even troubling. Sensitive and sustained support is vital in sustaining the school ethos.

Case study two: Music is why we come to school: Ramiro Solans School, Spain

The beat of a rumba escapes from the music room. The artists are Noé, on keyboard, and Pedro, bongos, from Primary 6. They are not put off by the presence of visitors – they're used to playing in public. Noé assures us proudly, "We've performed many times because of this song." The Rumba of Peace has become famous across the city of Zaragoza in the many districts where they have performed. The school development initiative "Motivational strategies – interdisciplinary projects through music, visual art and drama" won a special award in the competition organised by publisher Santillana. This is one of several development programmes at Ramiro Solans School.

The street mix
The district has a very high proportion of Gypsy families and recent immigrants of different nationalities, as well as native Spaniards. There is a great mix in the streets, but not in the schools. In this neighbourhood there is a high school, two state elementary schools – Ramiro Solans and King Ferdinand the Catholic – and a privately run convent school, which is always oversubscribed and the preferred option for indigenous Spaniards. The other children divide between Ramiro Solans and King Ferdinand, with a large Gypsy population in both but especially Ramiro Solans. Alfredo Molina, recently the school's headteacher, explains[1]:

> This is the Gypsies' School. That's what people call it, and that's what it is. We have 130 pupils, of whom 75 percent are from Gypsy families, 20 percent immigrants and the other 5 percent Spanish. But you have to realise that we receive the very poorest Gypsies – only one market trader – the rest survive on social security and what they can find.

Absenteeism and poor behaviour have been a major barrier to children's progress – the motivational strategies aim to take advantage of what they enjoy in order to engage them. The principal teacher for creative arts, Armando Carmona, explains:

> We started these projects in 2001-02 as an educational response to our pupils. We did some research to discover what our pupils needed and what motivated them. When I first came to this school four years ago, 90 percent of the pupils were of Gypsy background, and the rest of other nationalities. We decided to work out some basic principles and strategies to convince them to come to school. At that time, absenteeism was 50 percent. Now it is 10 to 12 percent. Studying their needs showed us a set of very basic problems, such as hygiene, unhealthy diet and leisure activities, a lack of respect for basic norms of behaviour, poor work habits, low self-esteem, poor concentration,

a limited vocabulary and so on. On the positive side, in terms of potential motivation, we found a taste for manual activities, visual language, computers, story telling, drama, songs and games, pets and the world of animals – and they wanted to appear in any way possible in the regional newspaper.

The teachers knew they had to fulfil certain basic needs in order to help the children succeed in life, but the key principle they arrived at was clear: that they could only fulfil the needs if they focused on the motivation. They concluded that creative and performing arts were the key. Armando Carmona continues:

> Music in particular is central to our pupils' culture and motivation. By using resources such as songs and dance, computers, games and festivals, among others, the pupils participate and engage – they feel that they are active players, individually and cooperatively. And all of this develops self-esteem, which seems to us to be fundamental, as well as working habits, concentration and motivation. And besides, it is the bridge towards working in other areas of the curriculum.
>
> The idea emerged of an organic curriculum design. The central aspects, to which everything connects, are music, visual arts and drama. These lead out to other parts of the curriculum: mathematics, environmental and social studies, religion, physical education, language and English. They also help the school to link with other organisations: the health centre, the community association, the Gypsy Association of Zaragoza, the regional newspaper, the leisure centre, the senior citizens' centre and the local Learning Community, a cooperative network of schools and education centres in the town.

"A festival every month"

The curriculum is now organised as a series of whole-school monthly projects based on seasonal festivities. In October it is Pilar (the Virgin of the Rock), in November autumn, with chestnuts ripening, then Christmas, in January the festival of peace, then Carnival followed by spring, Aragon's regional festival in April, the school's cultural week in May and in June a ceremony to say goodbye to the school leavers. "It's a matter of judging what is going to interest and engage the pupils, and taking advantage of that."

All the classes are involved in these projects in different ways, with diverse roles according to the age group. The creative and performing arts teachers started off by designing units with particular objectives and content, and a brief explanation of activities and how they can relate to other curriculum areas. These were then developed cooperatively with the tutors for each level, and taking account also of the other local agencies and groups.

Each unit lasts around a month, until the work is exhibited and performed in an open afternoon for parents, with dances, poetry, dramatic performance and an exhibition of all kinds of other work.

This is a very important way for parents to get involved in the school, and particularly because of our pupils' characteristics. Some teachers objected – they didn't like the fuss and confusion, they said it was too much like a street parade – but the pupils insisted: "We like our families coming to see what we do at school. We like them hearing us sing and seeing that we're real artists."

Arts education has been very strong for some years. This is why the school is so colourful: every wall, every corridor is decorated with paintings and designs. You walk along and suddenly encounter false doors like those of Zaragoza's Aljaferia Palace. Around the corner, the wall is decorated to look like the city's Roman wall. This arose from the most recent project, a study of Roman and Muslim Zaragoza. It was the backdrop for dances and drama to take the pupils back to that period. The experience helped to engage them in the history of their city.

Learning poetry and solidarity through the words of a song
Each teacher dedicates some class time to working on the monthly project, alongside aspects of the regular subject curriculum. The small class size makes it easier to implement different strategies: flexible grouping, using different resources and motivational materials – IT, audiovisual materials, stories and games – as well as workshop sessions and a pace that is adjusted to the pupils' working rhythms and can engage them actively.

The music teacher writes or adapts a song for each unit. As Armando Carmona explains:

We try to use a wide range of multicultural genres, as a way to connect with the world. They are passionate about rumba, but we also use jazz, reggae, rap, waltzes, traditional music and so on. The song and its dance are fundamental to the project. In the music class we work on the words, the rhythm, the score, the instrumentation. Some pupils already know how to play an instrument, and others learn here. We learn and practise dance steps, adapted to the age of pupils. Music becomes a real motor of learning.

The kids get involved so they're motivated to learn other things. For example, in the Pilar festival, we make large heads, and that involves all kinds of learning, not only modelling – we use mathematics and explore different units of measurement. Using karaoke with a copy of the lyrics is a great way to get them reading and writing, and we have used a song from Liberia as the starting point to study the war in that country. The song lyrics enable you to experiment with poetry, but also include information, whether it's the months of autumn, for the youngest children, or what happens in nature during autumn. A very open starting point was the theme "I wish", in which they expressed a desire to get rid of dictators around the world. They decided every child should have a rabbit instead of a gun.

We use computers to input the words. Whatever it is, they learn enthusiastically. But also, because they enjoy taking part in the projects, this develops values such as responsibility and respect as norms of behaviour. The pupils know that in order to take part in the final performance they have to follow certain norms of behaviour, and if not, they just won't be able to participate. There have been cases when the main performer of a song or drama has been replaced by another pupil or even a teacher – they know what will happen and take it very seriously. But I believe that the most important aspect of these projects is that the children are happy at school – they like coming to school now.

Noé and Pedro, the artists of the day, agree. They say it's the best school in the world, just a bit different from the others, and that the teachers really work hard to teach them. Both insist that going to school is really important because you can learn there. Noé and Pedro each want to fulfil their ambitions when they leave school: to repair televisions and to be a stockbreeder.

One big project and others under way

The reality of working at the school, frustrating for some teachers but engaging for all, led them to replan the standard curriculum and adapt it to their pupils' characteristics, their problems and their environment. There is a staff of 18, including a qualified psychologist, two learning support teachers, a specialist in therapeutic pedagogy and a teacher of religion. They work closely with outside agencies, such as health and social services, on the health programme, which involves promoting personal hygiene and safety, and ensuring vaccinations and dental checks.

Noé, the boy who was so keen to play for us, points out another important school development: "In other schools there are occasional trips out, and just for one class. Here the whole school goes out together."

As one of the teachers explains:

Such visits are a very important part of the curriculum here, since many of our children have never been outside the neighbourhood; they have never seen beyond these streets. If it weren't for the school, these children would never get to the theatre.

Notes

Introduction

1 Eduardo Galeano, *Upside Down: a Primer for the Looking-Glass World* (New York, Metropolitan Books, 2000). This outstanding and thought-provoking book on the culture and politics of life in our time is written from a Latin American perspective but has global relevance.
2 See Brian Simon, *Studies in the History of Education 1780-1870* (Lawrence and Wishart, 1960). This is the first volume of an excellent series.
3 For further information and sources, see Chapter 7.
4 There are many examples in the Key Stage 3 Strategy.
5 Rethinking Schools' website *www.rethinkingschools.org* contains online editions of its magazine, criticism of government policies, and other information and ideas.
6 An introduction to Scotland's proposed curriculum reform A Curriculum for Excellence can be found at *www.scotland.gov.uk/library5/education/cerv-00.asp*
7 I would also like to thank my colleagues at Edinburgh University who have made significant contributions, especially Gwynedd Lloyd and George Hunt, without whom Chapters 5 and 7 could not have been written. There have been many less direct influences, including Douglas Barnes whose work on classroom language and the curriculum planted many seeds; the teachers I observed when gathering material for my first book *The Power to Learn: S tories of Success in the Education of Asian and Other Bilingual Pupils* (Trentham, 2000), who remain an inspiration; and the enlightened campaigns of the teacher unions and the socialist movement.

Chapter 1 Tested to destruction

1 David Taylor, director of inspection at Ofsted, reported in the *Independent*, 13 March 2003. He added that working class boys in particular had become the "unwitting casualties" of the government's testing regime because of this. See www.literacytrust.org.uk/Database/stats/leagueindex.html
2 This report appears at www.literacytrust.org.uk/Pubs/sainsbury.html

3 This comes from PISA (Programme for International Student Assessment), a survey organised by the OECD, covering over 30 countries. Though misused by some politicians as a way of putting pressure on schools, it has produced extensive data and some illuminating analyses.

4 The Toronto team's evaluation of the literacy strategy *Watching and Learning 2* is available at www.standards.dfes.gov.uk/literacy/publications. The inspectorate's report National Literacy Strategy: the third year (2001) can be found on the Ofsted website *www.Ofsted.gov.uk*

5 This prestigious and authoritative journal is run by the British Educational Research Association to which most university staff in this field belong.

6 *British Educational Research Journal*, October 2003.

7 As above, August 2004.

8 Mary Hilton, "Are the Key Stage 2 Reading Tests becoming Easier Each Year?", *Reading*, no.1 (2001). This journal has now been renamed *Literacy*, see www. ukla.org

9 *National Literacy Strategy: the Third Year*

10 *Guardian*, 24 January 2006: "Children are less able than they used to be."

11 This is not entirely conclusive. Only 61 percent of the original chosen sample responded, and others had to be substituted. The number of pupils in each school who sat the test was also low. In the 2003 round, the take-up in England was so low that Britain was excluded from the final report. There may be a greater tendency for under-performing schools to avoid taking part.

12 From 2007 the "five or more A* to C grades or equivalent" benchmark will also require a certificate in English and maths.

13 Information for many different countries is on the OECD website www.oecd.org

14 An interesting analysis appears in a chapter by Andy Hargreaves, "Professional Learning Communities and Performance Training Cults: the Emerging Apartheid of School Improvement", in A Harris and others, *Effective Leadership for School Improvement* (RoutledgeFalmer, 2003)

15 The Assessment Reform Group's papers can be found at http://arg.educ.cam.ac.uk/

16 Rich tasks are part of Queensland's exciting New Basics initiative. An explanation and many examples can be found at http://education.qld.gov. au/corporate/newbasics/

Chapter 2   Full-spectrum surveillance

1 Some of the material in this chapter first appeared in chapter 3 of T Wrigley, *Schools of Hope: a New Agenda for School Improvement* (Trentham Books, 2003) where an extended discussion is to be found.

2 The Thatcher government shied away from privatising school inspection in Scotland, where they had little support, and HMI continued to operate as a professional body, though sometimes imitating the authoritarian tone south of the border.

3 In its Blairite rhetoric, the white paper promises to "raise the bar on underperformance". "*Satisfactory*" no longer means good enough; "satisfactory will be a demanding standard, and will not be awarded where there are any

aspects of unsatisfactory". Twisting language, the white paper condemns schools that are *"only* satisfactory". The intention is clearly to accelerate the closure and subsequent privatisation of schools.

4 Reported on the BBC website http://news.bbc.co.uk/1/hi/education/1924203.stm

5 The British Educational Research Association held a special seminar to scrutinise the research on "effective teaching" commissioned by the DfES. Some of the conclusions are summarised in *Research Intelligence*, no 76.

6 The quotations used here come from P Clarke, "Feeling Compromised – the Impact on Teachers of the Performance Culture", *Improving Schools*, 4/3 (2001); M Fielding, "Target Setting, Policy Pathology and Student Perspectives: Learning to Labour in New Times", *Cambridge Journal of Education*, 29/2 (1999); R Sennett *The Corrosion of Character: the Personal Consequences of Work in the New Capitalism* (W W Norton, 1998); C Mitchell and L Sackney *Profound Improvement: Building Capacity for a Learning Community* (Swets and Zeitlinger, 2000). Also worth reading are M Fielding (ed) *Taking Education Really Seriously: Four Years Hard Labour* (RoutledgeFalmer, 2001), and P Mahony and I Hextall *Reconstructing Teaching: Standards, Performance and Accountability* (RoutledgeFalmer, 2000).

7 For Fred Inglis's work on managerialism in education, see for example: "Managerialism and Morality" in W Carr, *Quality in Teaching* (RoutledgeFalmer, 1989), and "A Malediction Upon Management", *Journal of Education Policy*, 15/4 (2000).

8 John Macbeath's recent books (with co-authors, all published by Routledge) include: *Schools Must Speak for Themselves* (1999), *Self-Evaluation in European Schools* (2000), *Self-Evaluation in the Global Classroom* (2003)

9 Some of the work of the Cesar Chavez Institute can be studied at www.idea.gseis.ucla.edu/

Chapter 3   Improving schools – or speeding up the conveyor belt?

1 International comparisons are always problematic, but the OECD's PISA research is probably more reliable than its predecessors, both in terms of the assessment instruments themselves and the quality of the research studies analysing the results.

2 Heywood Community High School had been under so much pressure from competing schools that it would doubtless have been closed in the early 1990s but for the determination of the ward councillor and chair of education who felt that the council estate had to have its own community school.

3 T Wrigley, *The Power to Learn.*

4 Some of the arguments in this chapter can be found, in greater detail, in Chapters 1 and 2 of T Wrigley, *Schools of Hope.* Also T Wrigley (2004) "School Effectiveness – the Problem of Reductionism", *British Educational Research Journal*, 30/2 (2004). Further critiques can be found in L Morley and N Rassool *School Effectiveness: Fracturing the Discourse* (Falmer, 1999) and R Slee and G Weiner, (eds) *School Effectiveness for Whom?* (Falmer, 1998).

5 J S Coleman and others, *Equality of Educational Opportunity* (Washington DC:

Government Printing Office, 1966).

6 C Teddlie and D Reynolds in the journal *School Effectiveness and School Improvement*, 12/1 (2001), pp70-71.

7 P Mortimore and G Whitty, *Can School Improvement Overcome the Effects of Disadvantages?* (London Institute of Education, 1997). Peter Mortimore led a team which produced one of the most interesting studies of inner London schools, based on extended observations as well as statistical data. He is seen as one of the pioneers of school effectiveness, but his vision and methodology are broader and more enlightened.

8 Recently a new approach (the Index of Multiple Deprivation) has been developed in Scotland, based on population characteristics of small geographical areas. It is better able to reflect the circumstances of the whole pupil population.

9 See especially D Gillborn and H Mirza, *Educational Inequality: Mapping Race, Class and Gender* (2000), available at www.Ofsted.gov.uk

10 www.pisa.oecd.org

11 A translation of key parts of the German analysis of PISA appears in *Improving Schools*, 5/3 (2002).

12 See, for example, H Gunter, *Leaders and Leadership in Education* (Chapman, 2001); M Thrupp and R Willmott, *Education Management in Managerialist Times* (Open University, 2003); S Gewirtz, *The Managerial School* (Routledge, 2002).

13 These quotations come from articles based on school visits, *Improving Schools*, 5/2 and 4/1.

14 Maud Blair and Jill Bourne's report *Making the Difference* (1998) appears to have disappeared from government websites, but a print version is published by Prentice Hall / Harvester Wheatsheaf (1999).

15 T Wrigley, *The Power to Learn*, provides a very different explanation from official versions of school improvement. The book is the result of observation and interviews in ten different schools, with many examples of interesting teaching and community engagement.

Chapter 4 Dividing communities, privatising schools

1 These details come from a pamphlet by Tony Edwards and Sally Tomlinson, *Selection isn't Working* (Catalyst, 2002). See www.catalystforum.org. uk/pubs/paper11.html). The pamphlet presents an excellent defence of comprehensive education. In Clyde Chitty and Brian Simon's *Promoting Comprehensive Education in the 21st Century* (Trentham, 2001) many different writers express their opposition to New Labour's abandonment of the comprehensive principle.

2 Significant information is now emerging from Finland, including an evaluation by the OECD's PISA research team, *The Finnish Success in PISA – and Some Reasons Behind it* (www.pisa.oecd.org). Although there are problems in making international comparisons fairly, PISA has produced a substantial database and enabled thoughtful researchers to consider possible influences on achievement,

rather than automatically assuming that a correlation amounts to a pattern of cause and effect.

3 Two leading members of the German research team, B Baumert and G Schümer, summarise aspects of their PISA report in *Improving Schools*, 5/2 (2002).

4 Incidentally, it is a myth to suggest that parents had no choice before the late 1980s. In Scotland today it is still the presumption that children will attend the local school, but they can opt for a different one when there is room.

5 This has gone on for many years, though backbench MPs insisted on it being outlawed in the 2006 Education and Inspections Bill. Once enough schools are privatised as "trust schools", such a ban is unlikely to hold. In fact, the London Oratory School attended by Tony Blair's children won a court case on the grounds that it was extremely popular and needed to select pupils on the basis of their religious fervour.

6 Diane Reay writes about the efforts of more advantaged families to secure greater success for their children within a competitive school system in *Improving Schools*, 5/2 (2002).

7 Another government myth is that the facility for 14 to 16 year olds to pursue a specialist course at a further education college is their own recent invention. At the comprehensive school where I worked in the early 1970s, students were able to attend construction and hairdressing courses a day a week at the college, alongside a broad school-based curriculum.

8 www.eis.org.uk/html/news/nr25may04.htm

9 Increasingly damning evidence is emerging about the government's flagship Academies project. The transcript of BBC Radio 4's *File on 4* programme (23 November 2004) can be found at http://news.bbc.co.uk/1/hi/programmes/file_on_4/3708232.stm. A comprehensive source is the NUT website www.teachers.org.uk (search for Academies)

10 The data of 2001 has been chosen as a baseline for these three schools, rather than 2002, to avoid the distorting effect of impending closure on exam results. It is always possible that results will suffer when students and teachers know that their school is about to close.

11 These results derive from comparing the academies' 2005 results with the 2002 results of the schools they replaced. Taking on trust the "equivalence" of GNVQ intermediate with four GCSEs at grade C or above, we find that the percentage gaining "five A* to Cs or the equivalent" rose from 23 percent at the old schools to 37 percent at the academies. But if we count the GNVQ as equivalent to only a single GCSE subject, the change would be far smaller – from 20 percent of pupils gaining "the equivalent" of five good GCSEs to 22 percent.

12 A shift from 14.3 percent to 14.9 percent would amount to more than three students, but for the fact that the overall number of final year pupils at the academies is smaller than it was at the predecessor schools. In part this is due to less successful pupils being expelled from the academies.

13 See *The Business of Education Improvement* published by the CBI in February 2005. Page 10 lists the many different ways in which businesses make profits from education budgets. This revealing document insists that much more than the

present third of schools' budgets should become a source of profit. It proposes that successful education authorities should also be privately run, and not only the more risky ones which are an uncertain source of profit.

14 The Scottish research comparing attainment in state and independent schools is summarised in *Improving Schools* 5/3, with more substantial data at www. institute-of-governance.org (the researcher was L Paterson).

Chapter 5   Standardised schools, excluded students

1 The term *Medical model* is a little unfortunate, since current medical education now emphasises social causes of ill health.

2 There is a growing literature on the misinterpretation of Black pupils' behaviour, and on exclusions from school, for example M Blair, *Why Pick on Me?* (Trentham, 2001); T Sewell, *Black Masculinities and Schooling* (Trentham, 1997) and see the chapters from the UK and US in R Majors, (ed), *Educating our Black Children: New Directions and Radical Approaches* (RoutledgeFalmer, 2001). A much broader discussion of the school experience of African-Caribbean pupils can be found in the recent book edited by Brian Richardson, (ed), *Tell it Like It Is: How Our Schools Fail Black Children* (Bookmarks / Trentham Books, 2005).

3 K Riley and E Rustique-Forrester, *Working with Disaffected Students: Why Students Lose Interest and What We Can Do About It* (Sage, 2003).

4 The main source for this section is an excellent new book by G Lloyd, J Stead and D Cohen, *Critical New Perspectives on ADHD* (RoutledgeFalmer, 2006).

5 The list of symptoms was downloaded from the US Department of Health's website: www.cdc.gov, and based on the DSM-IV *Diagnostic and Statistical Manual of Mental Disorders* (Fourth Edition). The accompanying notes include the advice that doctors should rely on reports from teachers or parents, as they are unlikely to see the evidence directly.

6 See 4 above, chapter by D Cohen.

7 The quotation is from Armstrong's chapter in G Lloyd and others, *Critical New Perspectives on ADHD*, as above.

Chapter 6   Community and democracy

1 There are many examples in T Wrigley, *The Power to Learn*.

2 There is no English source for the conference, "School is a house of learning". Its discussions are available in German: Bildungskommission NRW, *Zukunft der Bildung – Schule der Zukunft* (Neuwied, 1995).

3 The schools are Blakeston Community School and Spittal Primary School (report in the journal *Improving Schools*, 4/1, 2001)

4 A special issue of *Forum: for Promoting 3-19 Comprehensive Education*, 43/2 (Summer 2001) was devoted to the theme of student voice. The questions derive from Michael Fielding's concluding article, "Beyond the Rhetoric of Student Voice".

5 See T Wrigley and N Fjeld Lofsnaes, "Schools as Social and Learning Communities",

Improving Schools, 8/1 (2005)

6 The best starting point for examples and research is probably www. schoolredesign.net/

7 British secondary schools which have implemented alternative forms of organisation include Falinge Park, Rochdale (in T Wrigley, *The Power to Learn*) and the recently opened and purpose-built Bishops Park College, Clacton. The longest-standing example is probably Stantonbury Campus, Milton Keynes. Further information can be found at www.hse.org.uk including the campaign by some independent small schools to become state-funded.

8 The best source is Pierre Bourdieu, "The Forms of Capital", in A H Halsey and other, *Education – Culture, Economy, Society* (CUP, 1997). Bourdieu's essay is also available in other anthologies.

9 In L Moll (ed), *Vygotsky and Education* (Cambridge, 1990).

10 www.cecip.com.br

11 For this and other examples, see P Thomson, "Miners, Diggers, Ferals and Show-Men: School-Community Projects that Affirm and Unsettle Identities and Place", *British Journal of Sociology of Education*, 27 (1) (2006).

12 The story of the Edible Schoolyard can be found, along with many other innovative projects, on www.edutopia.org. This website contains a video report of this and the other projects.

Chapter 7   'Literacy' is just not good enough

1 I am not proposing realism in the sense of simply mirroring reality, since fantasy and play are vital in enabling us to see the world differently and explore alternatives. They provide the opportunity for engaged participation in an imagined world.

2 A number of research reports have revealed how the literacy hour limits pupils' spoken language in the classroom, including M Mroz, F Smith and F Hardman, "The Discourse of the Literacy Hour", *Cambridge Journal of Education*, 30/3; E English, L. Hargreaves and J Hislam, 'Pedagogical Dilemmas in the National Literacy Strategy", *Cambridge Journal of Education* 32/1, (2002); C Burns and D Myhill, 'Interactive or Inactive? a Consideration of the Nature of Interaction in Whole Class Teaching', *Cambridge Journal of Education*, 34/1 (2004) and F Smith, F Hardman, K Wall and M Mroz, "Interactive Whole Class Teaching in the National Literacy and Numeracy Strategies" (*British Educational Research Journal*, 30/3 (2004).

3 Philip Pullman's *Isis Lecture* (1 April 2003), www.philip-pullman.com

4 Claims made on behalf of "synthetic phonics" based on the Clackmannanshire experiment can be read at *www.scotland.gov.uk/library5/education/ins17-00.asp*. Wendy Berliner's article in the *Guardian* (5 April 2005) shows flaws in the argument, especially when regarded as a panacea. http://education.guardian. co.uk/egweekly/story/0,5500,1451842,00.html The Literacy Trust provides links to key articles www.literacytrust.org.uk/ Database/Primary/phonics.html

5 *Reading for Purpose and Pleasure* can be found on www.Ofsted.gov.uk/publications

6 The extract from Jim Cummins and the quote from James Moffet are both from Jim Cummins's chapter in P Trionfas, *Pedagogies of Difference* (RoutledgeFalmer, 2003).

7 The quotations in this section are from Bethan Marshall's chapter, "English Teachers and the Third Way" in Brian Cox (ed), *Literacy is Not Enough – Essays on the Importance of Reading* (Manchester University Press, 1998). The book is an excellent collection of critical writings on government literacy policy.

8 *Observer*, 7 February 1982.

9 Paulo Freire's books range from literacy in rural areas (from the 1970s) to his work in the city of Sao Paulo in the 1990s. The best known early works include *Pedagogy of the Oppressed* (Penguin, 1996, originally published 1970) and *Cultural Action for Freedom* (Harvard Educational Review, 1970).

10 A recent book for teachers illustrating how Shakespeare can be studied from diverse perspectives is A Fellowes, *Bilingual Shakespeare* (Trentham, 2001)

11 The English and Media Centre (www.englishandmedia.co.uk) is an outstanding source of creative teaching ideas. The ideas on opening texts are in M Simons and E Plackett, *The English Curriculum: Reading 1– Comprehension* (The English and Media Centre) which is still available.

12 In T Wrigley, *The Power to Learn*.

13 The ideas on critical literacy derive from:
B Comber and A Simpson (eds), *Negotiating Critical Literacies in the Classroom* (Erlbaum, 2001);
J Evans (ed), *Literacy Moves on* (Fulton, 2004);
M Straker-Wells (ed), *Education for a Multicultural Society – Case Studies in ILEA Schools* (Bell and Hyman, 1984);
S Robbins and M Dyer(eds), *Writing America – Classroom Literacy and Public Engagement* (Teachers College Press, 2003).

Chapter 8 Curriculum, class and globalisation

1 This new book, full of practical examples, can be obtained from www.rethinkingschools.org

2 R Johnson, "Really Useful Knowledge", in J Clarke and others (eds), *Working-Class Culture: Studies in History and Theory* (Hutchinson, 1979).

3 There are dangers in this argument, if it is assumed that barriers to access mean intellectual weakness. Some reactionary writers have argued that working-class pupils should be educated in different schools, with a curriculum which is rich in experience but poor in ideas. The most notorious was G H Bantock, one of the authors of the *Black Papers on Education,* basing his thinking on extracts from D H Lawrence. See C B Cox and A E Dyson (eds), *The Black Papers: Vol. 1-111* (Critical Quarterly Society, 1971).

4 Revolutionary Russian psychologist Lev Semyonovic Vygotsky made exactly this point in chapter 7 of his *Thinking and Speech* (MIT, 1962): "The teacher achieves nothing but a mindless learning of words, an empty verbalism...the child learns not the concept but the word, and...through memory rather than thought.

It substitutes the learning of dead and empty verbal schemes for the master of living knowledge."

5 The fraudulence of this view was thoroughly exposed by Stephen J Gould, Steven Rose and others.

6 A summary account of how concepts such as "intelligence" and "language deficit" have been deployed can be found in T Wrigley, *Schools of Hope*, ch 5. Earlier sources include W Cowburn, *Class, Ideology and Community Education* (Croom Helm, 1986) and S Rose and others (1984) *Not in Our Genes* (Penguin, 1984).

7 In fact, as Bernstein conceded, they are not related to one particular social group: "Tea, dear?" makes perfect sense in the right context, without a verb.

8 See B Bernstein, *Class, Codes and Control* (Routledge).

9 W Labov, *The Logic of Non-Standard English* (1969), is available in various anthologies including P Giglioli, *Language and Social Context* (Penguin, 1972); Harold Rosen, *Language and Class* (Falling Wall Press, 1972).

10 The prime stimulus for this section came from E Wenger, *Communities of Practice* (CUP, 1998), p34.

11 Wenger prefers the term *reification*, which could be confusing but implies an ability to step back from an experience, focus and crystallize. He argues for a dialectical unity between the two poles of participation and reification.

12 L Vygotsky, *Thinking and Speech*, as above, ch 7: "By learning algebra, the child comes to understand arithmetic operations as particular instantiations of algebraic operations. This gives the child a freer, more abstract and generalised view of his operations with concrete quantities."

13 J Bruner, Two Modes of Thought, in his *Actual Minds, Possible Worlds* (Harvard University Press, 1968).

14 P Adey and M Shayer, *Really Raising Standards* (Routledge, 1994).

15 The examples are from T Wrigley, *The Power to Learn*.

16 J Cummins, *Bilingualism and Special Education: Issues in Assessment and Pedagogy* (College HillPress, 1984), and *Negotiating Identities: Education for Empowerment in a Diverse Society* (California Assoc for Bilingual, 1996).

17 www.dfes.gov.uk/publications/5yearstrategy/

Chapter 9   What should Citizenship really look like?

1 One education minister decreed that history lessons should not deal with anything more recent than 25 years ago. In 2006 that would mean not teaching that the Cold War and apartheid had finished.

2 Even under Thatcher, schools had a responsibility for pupils' "Spiritual, Moral, Social and Cultural Development", a phrase from the 1988 Education Reform Act, which some influential inspectors had insisted should be part of school inspections. Often this was tokenistic and conformist, with moral and social development seen as teaching good behaviour, but many schools were able to develop far more critical versions. All ten case study schools in my first book, *The Power to Learn*, provide inspiring examples.

3 Illogically, the word *vocational* does not tend to be used for a degree in medicine or law.
4 S Kemmis, P Cole and D Suggett, *Orientations to Curriculum and Transition: Towards the Socially Critical School* (Victorian Institute of Secondary Education, Melbourne, 1983)
5 The Rose Gentle video can be obtained or downloaded from the Military Families Against the War website, www.mfaw.org.uk/resources.html
6 A video of this project can be found on Teachers' TV.
7 Chris Searle's courageous struggle to develop a radical version of English teaching can be found in various of his books, with many inspiring examples, for example *Classrooms of Resistance* (Writers and Readers, 1975).
8 Philip Wexler, "Structure, text and subject: a critical sociology of school knowledge", in M Apple, *Cultural and Economic Reproduction in Education* (Routledge, 1982). He argues that these are systematically absent from most school learning, along with habits of teaching and learning which discourage critical questions (ie the assumption that the textbook and the teacher present a single authoritative truth).
9 www.highwire.org.uk This website contains some outstanding projects on colonialism, fair trade, DNA testing, earthquakes and civil rights.
10 Raymond Williams's published work is enormous and of ongoing significance. Good starting points are *Culture and Society 1780-1950* (Chatto & Windus, 1958); *The Country and the City* (Chatto & Windus, 1973); *The English Novel from Dickens to Lawrence* (Chatto & Windus, 1970).
11 See note 6.
12 See end of Chapter 1.
13 From a Danish government publication, *Samfundsfag* (ie Social Education, or Education for Citizenship), in 1995.
14 The declaration, known as the *Beutelsbach Consensus*, is in S Schiele and H Schneider, *Das Konsensproblem in der Politischen Bildung* (Wehling, 1977). An English translation is available at www.lpb.bwue.de/beutels.htm#english
15 The international Storyline Network holds annual conferences, and shares ideas through www.storyline.org. Other material can be found at www.acskive.dk/storyline.
16 The concept of design challenges was first developed at the University of Syracuse (US), where it was known as Education by Design. It is supported in Britain by Critical Skills (www.criticalskills.co.uk).

Conclusion: Resistance and renewal

I would like to thank Jon Berry of the Anti-SATs Alliance for his extensive contributions to this chapter.

1 ATL press release, 1 December 2003
2 *Education Guardian*, 21 August 2003
3 Her Majesty's Chief Inspector of Schools: Annual Report 2001-2

4 *Why We Must Stop the SATs*, available from information@rethinkinged.org.uk

5 The Centre was originally run by the Inner London Education Authority, which Margaret Thatcher's government decided to close down. The teachers running the centre managed to remove everything in the middle of the night to it going as an independent organisation, and it is still thriving.

6 The various websites are easy to find using a search engine, and invariably publish more exciting resources than government departments.

7 Rethinking Education, and its website www.rethinkinged.org.uk will develop very quickly, thanks to the contribution you are about to make.

Appendix: Other schools, other places

1 Headteachers in many parts of Spain are elected from within the staff by their colleagues, usually serving for three or four years.

TELL IT LIKE IT IS:
How our schools fail Black children

bookmarks

Bookmarks is Britain's leading socialist bookshop, just around the corner from the TUC and the British Museum

We stock a huge range of books
- anti-racism and black struggle
- education and trade union resources
- anti-war and anti-imperialism
- classic and contemporary Marxism
- excellent children's section plus radical fiction, art and culture
- videos, audio CDs and political journals, together with a well stocked second hand section
- and much more

Our trade union book service provides comprehensive bookstalls for conferences. We are official booksellers to the TUC.

Any book in print can be ordered through us, and we have a full mail order service.

Bookmarks, 1 Bloomsbury Street, London WC1B 3QE
020 7637 1848
www.bookmarks.uk.com

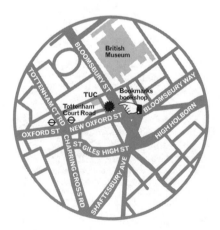